ADVANCE PRAISE

"There are few individuals whose single-handed advice, counsel, and support are catalytic to the growth of a company—providing it the fuel that it needs to break through the atmosphere and make it into the galaxy. Barbara Clarke is one of those people. She understands how to start and build companies, but she also understands the ecosystem and how to help founders successfully navigate it. I can definitively say that were it not for Barbara Clarke, there would have been no Angel Round, no Seed Round, no Series A round, and no company. Having Barbara as an investor and advisor are the greatest gifts that both founders and companies could ever receive."

—TANYA VAN COURT, CEO AND FOUNDER OF GOALSETTER

"As a CEO, founder, and serial VC-backed entrepreneur, I've experienced firsthand how critical your company's board of directors can be to your success or failure. Clarke's Build Your Board, Build Your Business provides founders with insights and strategies for sourcing the experienced individuals and mentors that will catapult your business to success."

—KIM FOLSOM, FOUNDER, CHAIRPERSON, CEO
OF FOUNDERS FIRST CAPITAL PARTNERS

"*The most successful entrepreneurs know how to inspire and when to listen. Build Your Board, Build Your Business is a smart, engaging, and essential book for any entrepreneur looking to leverage the power of listening, connection, and insight by building an effective and productive board of directors.*"

—L. GENNARI, ESQ., PARTNER AT GENNARI ARONSON, LLP
AND BOOK COLUMNIST FOR *Boston Business Journal*

"*For any startup founder or soon-to-be founder, Build Your Board, Build Your Business provides invaluable guidance and insights into an often overlooked part of starting a company—governance. Clarke breaks down the daunting task of building and managing a board with a clever and relatable approach, which any startup at any level can use.*"

—ELI VELASQUEZ, MANAGING PARTNER
OF INVESTORS OF COLOR

"*As a startup lawyer of thirty years I've experienced these issues firsthand hundreds of times and appreciate the practical guidance Barbara offers. She articulates the need for a vibrant, supportive board, provides exactly the right context for the role of the board, and demystifies the process for making a strong board a core component of building a successful high-growth company. Build Your Board, Build Your Business is a gift I send to all of my startup CEOs!*"

—MATT KIRMAYER, ESQ., PARTNER AT PERKINS COIE LLC

"*A strong and strategic board can significantly increase the trajectory of a company. Barbara has successfully guided, mentored, challenged, and lifted countless companies as an investor and as a seasoned board member. Build Your Board, Build Your Business is a foundational guide for any founder looking to grow their business.*"

—CORDERO BARKLEY, PARTNER AND DIRECTOR OF
FINANCE AND INVESTMENTS AT TITLETOWNTECH

BUILD YOUR BOARD,
BUILD YOUR BUSINESS

BUILD YOUR
BOARD,
BUILD YOUR
BUSINESS

The Path to Million Dollar Success Explained

BARBARA CLARKE

THE **IMPACT** SEAT
P U B L I S H I N G

BUILD YOUR BOARD, BUILD YOUR BUSINESS
The Path to Million Dollar Success Explained

FIRST EDITION

ISBN 978-1-5445-2575-4 *Hardcover*
      978-1-5445-2573-0 *Paperback*
      978-1-5445-2574-7 *Ebook*

To all those entrepreneurs who are trying to take the next great leap forward in their business. I hope you find this book a helpful guide through the forest. You do not need to go it alone.

CONTENTS

INTRODUCTION

A couple of years ago, I spoke with a successful CEO whose company had several million dollars in annual revenue. She called me to get feedback on some expansion ideas she had. In the course of the conversation, I was shocked to learn that she did not have an accountant on staff; an outsourced bookkeeper—who she thought was great—managed the finances of her multimillion dollar company. I also learned that the company didn't have a line of credit for their purchases of product despite their size and years of business.

As we continued to talk, she spoke of her vision and several ideas on how to take her business to the next level. She admitted she needed some advice, though. I told her that she needed to create a board of directors.

She had not created one before because she thought that boards were for bigger companies or for companies that got venture capital. She didn't realize until we spoke that a board of directors would be the special sauce she needed to take her company to the next level.

She didn't know how to begin to create a board of directors. Then and there, the idea for this book was formed. I want all CEOs to learn how to create a highly effective board of directors because it is the secret sauce to achieving their next level of success.

This book presents true stories from both my own experience and that of my peers and colleagues. While I've changed the names and some of the facts to protect the privacy of the people involved, I'm hoping this book provides enough transparency to make the process of creating a board a manageable endeavor. My goal is to demystify creating a board so all CEOs can take this on. And for those of you reading this who aren't the CEO yet, you will be well prepared when it is your time.

FRESH EYES

A company whose CEO I know well wanted to drum up sales for their new business venture, so they hired marketing people to create a website, conduct some public relations, and get the word out. The company was successful in creating awareness about their business, and their revenue increased as they began to attract more customers.

However, when they prepared their tax return at the end

of the year, they realized they hadn't been as profitable as expected. At the beginning of the following year, the company created a board of directors. At the first meeting, the board took the time to review the company's profit and loss (P&L) statement. A member of the new board who had extensive P&L experience brought a fresh perspective to evaluating the situation; she asked *Who is your largest customer? What is your most profitable service?* Those questions shone a light on the profitability problem. The CEO could not answer those questions, and everyone immediately understood that while the company was spending a lot of money on marketing and PR, they were reaching the wrong prospects. They needed to identify the kind of customer and the kind of service that would be most profitable. A strong board of directors offers this type of business-changing insight and governance.

Have you ever been hiking where you can see that there's a beautiful hill close by, but you don't know which path to take to get there? Is there even a path? You wish you had a guide to show you, or someone who's walked it before who can share their experience. You know there are many ways to get to the summit, but which way is right for you and your skills?

Your business is like that hill; you've reached your high point, but you know there's more...you've seen other businesses achieve more revenue and serve more markets. The truth is, you can't bring it to the next level without guidance. Imagine if you had your own board of directors, there to assist, guide you, and focus on you and your company. The value of this group cannot be overstated. They can show you the way forward with advice on where to go and, maybe as important, what pitfalls to avoid.

Board members do not become involved in the day-to-day workings of a company. They aren't doing the accounting, placing orders for supplies, or making sales calls. A board considers the business situation and analyzes it. They apply their knowledge, bring their experience and expertise, and they speak up about things they notice. Maybe inventory is too high, or the receivables are too long. Board members are not setting themselves up at a desk in the company and taking on the receivables problem for the CEO. They observe the situation then guide the CEO, who in turn needs to take action on the advice.

Many entrepreneurs outright reject the idea of a board of directors because they fear they will have to give up control of their company. They imagine a room full of stuffy, old men judging them for their mistakes and telling them how to run their company. Absolutely not! Instead, imagine having a group of specialists, laser focused on you and your company—a group specifically assembled to complement your talents with their expertise. Imagine not feeling alone in your ambition to grow your company but, rather, having stable support and great minds to brainstorm with. Imagine these people also care about your health and well-being, your priorities, and your family obligations, as they know those directly affect the company. My goal is to help you build the board of your dreams and avoid anything less. Yet, it's not a dream—it's an achievable reality.

Even though your company is ultimately unique, when it comes to business, most entrepreneurs need the same set of tools, discipline being the first. A board can help a CEO prioritize their efforts to achieve the most important results.

Implementing strong accounting and financial reporting before investing in a marketing campaign might be an example.

It's not about keeping you grounded. A board will bring you genuine advice and a different perspective on how to achieve your goals. To demonstrate how a board can help you grow, let's follow one company's progress before and after their board.

Tanya's company installed computer systems for small businesses with multiple locations. They had consistently been generating revenue in the mid-six figures for several years. She was the first person in her family to own their own business, and she felt successful. Tanya also knew there was more opportunity out there, but she didn't know how to access the opportunity and grow her business. She enrolled in a program that helped her build a small board of directors; she rightly believed bringing in and learning from a team of experts would help her reach her goals.

After looking at business operations and its financial structure, a few board members suggested the company diversify their streams of income to increase profits. The company depended on a "transactional mode" strategy; they installed a system for a client and moved on. The board encouraged Tanya to talk to her customers about other services they might need. She discovered most needed help installing and implementing other software, and those implementations happened throughout the year.

One of the board members asked Tanya to consider how she could convert some of her sales to a subscription model to meet the demands of those clients and create an ongoing revenue stream. The board also reviewed and made recommendations for the structure of her contracts. Clients who adhere to a month-to-month subscription for your service or product fulfillment provide reliable, ongoing income, although the client can interrupt the subscription at any time. This board recommended adopting a more favorable contractual agreement that provides business and revenue stability: clients sign a contract for an extended period of time, such as multiple months or years, and must give advance notice to cancel before the contract expires. While both options offer recurring income, contracts, by their nature, are a better business choice.

In observing the overall picture of the company, the board further discussed how to track unit costs. The company needed to know the precise profitability of each product line because new revenue streams are beneficial only if they are profitable! If the company offered discounts or promotions to close a sale, the board explained, those costs of doing business would need to be tracked against revenue to calculate final profitability.

Scaling the business would take an excessive amount of time and effort, if that CEO even thought to diversify in the first place. Then, implementing the strategy on their own, without the advice and guidance of the board, likely wouldn't have gone as smoothly as it did. Having a board of directors is not a silver bullet; it's a lot of hard work, but everything changes with this group of advisors guiding you toward success.

THE BOARD IMPACTS YOUR BUSINESS

It has been my pleasure to see over and over again the impact a board of directors has on a company. Since my early years at Tufts University, I've possessed a deep interest in numbers, the way the economy works, and what makes companies successful. This led to the pursuit of a bachelor's in quantitative economics and, later, to a full scholarship to attend Brandeis University's graduate program. There, I received my master's in international economics and finance, which led to my first job, at KPMG, where I witnessed the inner financial workings of companies and the practices that drive their profitability.

In my management consulting roles, I got to see up close the day-to-day operations of massive Fortune 100 companies as well as the rocket-fast growth of venture-backed startups.

I learned the most about company growth, however, when I started to serve on various boards of directors. I observed, firsthand, the advice of the board of directors being given, received, and implemented. Companies consistently experienced steady growth based on that advise-and-implement pattern. I learned that the true essence of board membership is in being an effective contributor in collaboration with other board members. After observing more than ten thousand companies during my thirty-year career, I've concluded that a good board of directors is the single change that continually propels the most successful ones forward. Conversely, a bad board of directors can damage a company.

In this book, you'll learn how you can take control and construct the board that you need. First, you'll assess your existing skills and resources then strategically determine the skills needed to fill gaps in your business. Next, you'll learn the significance of, and how to approach, effectively communicating when handling your board. Last, you'll plan the steps for working with the board once it is established.

My wish is to fast-track the scores of women entering business today. According to Forbes, the fastest growing segment of entrepreneurs is Black women. In addition, women over 40 who had careers in corporate America are starting to break out into their own businesses. These are vibrant, intelligent individuals who are changing the status quo, and they don't need a stale, old board; they need strategic board members and fresh, lively ideas. This is the board of directors you want to create for your business—and I'm here to show you how.

ANCHOR

The actual steps of finding and retaining a board can be recalled by remembering the acronym ANCHOR:

- Assess
- Network
- Communicate
- Honor Legal Duty
- Organize
- Refresh & Return

I've dedicated a chapter to each letter of the acronym to guide you through the steps of building a board of directors for your company. I've seen scores of CEOs succeed using the ANCHOR pattern, and I hope to hear of even more as you employ it. It is the best way of obtaining both a board and your own small army of support, connections, and in some cases, capital.

While your board of directors provides external support, the creation of the board begins with looking inward, with thinking about yourself before thinking about bringing in outside help.

Chapter 1

THE JOURNEY OF PURSUING A BOARD

Do you need a board of directors? To answer that question you want to think about where you stand on the map of your business journey.

Creating a board of directors helps you scale your business, solve strategic problems, and fill your own knowledge and skill gaps. If your company is growing fast with many opportunities, a board of directors can offer priceless and timely advice to help you filter and prioritize those opportunities. If you're at an inflection point—whether that means standing on the cusp of Series A investments or considering an exit strategy—here, too, a board of directors can help you wade through the priorities and decision-making. They can also provide a valid and varied network to facilitate those inflection points.

If you're just starting out with an idea for a product or service or have just a few customers, or you're a solopreneur, it's early in the game for you to think about building a board of directors. You do still want to develop your ideas, network and talk to people, and strategize for bringing your product to market and increasing sales and revenue. When you reach those milestones or inflection points, you'll be poised to create a board comprising the best advisors for your situation.

Many entrepreneurs hold the mindset that they have to hit a certain revenue number to justify a board of directors. Revenue isn't always the best indicator of a company's standing. I've invested in companies that have no revenue but do have a board of directors guiding the executives at the helm while the company develops new technologies and prepares to launch in the marketplace.

Bringing in a group of trusted advisors who have your company's health in their best interests at the pivotal moment of your business can mean the difference between good and great success. Entrepreneurs often believe they have to carry the weight of their business alone—they don't. A board of directors will share the load. Opening your mind to that idea is a step in the right direction. There are other mindset shifts that facilitate your success.

ADJUSTING YOUR MINDSET

I've identified ten general mindsets that tend to entrap entrepreneurs. It's a good idea to reflect on these issues and be confident in the following areas in general. Addressing or adjusting these mindsets becomes critical if you're on your way to engaging a board.

WORK ON THE BUSINESS, NOT IN THE BUSINESS

This may seem contrary, but it is *not* your place, as CEO of your company, to jump in and resolve everything. If there's a challenging situation with a customer, for instance, you may want to pick up the phone and call them to sort things out. The amount of time you spend working on that problem when it should be handled by a capable team takes away time you have to think about the big picture of your company. What do the next six months look like? Who will the next hire be? Can you meet the quarterly budget?

If your business is too dependent on your involvement in the day-to-day, you're never going to move beyond the price that you can charge for your personal services. As you transition into the demands of your executive role, you must recruit and retain a trustworthy, competent staff to handle difficulties as they arise. You might have to make some hard choices about your existing staff.

WORK/LIFE INTEGRATION

Many years ago, a member of my staff was in training for the Boston Marathon. It was winter in Boston, so daylight hours were scarce, and nights were especially cold. He came to me a couple of days in and requested longer lunch hours so he could train at a less-harsh time of day. I was completely sympathetic to his predicament. Lunch hours were extended, and we further arranged prolonged evening hours to accommodate his workload.

Simple courtesies, such as holding off sending an email or making a business call to a staff member who is out of the office, go a long way in building a team and usually result in a dedicated staff. Board members who have built teams and understand this dynamic will assist you in retaining staff in a fair and business-effective way.

THOUGHTFUL HIRING

A common occurrence when a company starts to grow quickly is to promote people who are working in key support roles. Sometimes the person flourishes in the new role, but often they are not suited to the new position, and they might show evidence of distress, such as a decline in quality of work and deliverables.

Hiring is time consuming, and a board can help focus efforts and expand talent pools. For several boards, I have interviewed candidates as an extra set of eyes when the core team is small.

If a promotion has been made and that person is not suited to the new position, fair practice would suggest that this is the time to expand and restructure the roles so that they can continue to contribute in a way that they are most effective. A board that is aligned with this value can help you navigate through this circumstance, recommend suitable hires, and pinpoint an effective restructuring process.

Fast-growing companies always confront the old adage "What got you here isn't going to keep you here," and that applies to staff hiring especially. The team you had when there were five of you is going to look different when you grow to fifty people.

I had a company recently that was filing for its IPO (initial public offering, or referred to as "going public") and the top finance person decided to leave the company. The company scrambled for financial help at a time when they needed someone to lean into that role. Ideally, a board can help you identify those positions that are most likely to turn over as you grow so you, as CEO, are not surprised.

TIME MANAGEMENT TOOLS

Managing your time along the journey may prove more challenging than you thought. If you're having an especially difficult time managing your schedule, there are time management apps that can help by passively monitoring what you're spending time on. Organizational apps might also be beneficial as they help keep all the moving parts of your life in one spot, on your phone or computer.

Whether you use a sophisticated productivity tool or an old school notebook, take all of the tasks you're trying to accomplish, and make a written plan of how you'll approach each one throughout the day, week, month, even through the year. Step back now and then and become aware of yourself, your habits, and your progress.

VALUE YOUR OWN TIME OFF

Several years ago, Wendy, a colleague of mine, had planned a weekend ski trip at Mount Sunapee with her family. As she was straightening her desk in preparation to leave for that trip, she was nearly in tears. A tax deadline was fast approaching, and she had a mountain of paperwork to get through by midweek. She'd been completely stressed over it for the last two weeks, and she couldn't seem to catch up. She obviously felt that going skiing was an enormous waste of time during this last crucial weekend.

When I pulled into the parking ramp the following Monday morning, Wendy's car was already there. I walked past her office, and she was calmly at her desk, a large coffee cup already in the trash. The entire atmosphere around her was different. She was calm and focused. Apparently, on her way down a particularly difficult slope, on her second day at Mount Sunapee, it dawned on her that all she needed to clear her desk was one full day. So she got herself to the office by 6:00 a.m., put an email out that she was not to be disturbed for any reason throughout the day, and she was already well on her way to completing the paperwork by the time I arrived.

Be sure to regularly and thoroughly decompress during time off, even if it means letting a call or email wait until Monday. If you don't recharge, you will lose productivity. It's a fact that many uninspired individuals have come up with their best ideas during time away from work.

In the media, especially the media focused on startups and entrepreneurship, there is a ridiculous focus on "work hard/play hard" which, to me, looks like justification for the absurd "play hard" indulgences of the elite of Silicon Valley. It has been my experience, after walking the halls of many coworking spaces occupied by venture-backed startups, that this "work hard" is more show than reality.

I prefer "work smarter not harder" as my philosophy. Studies show that people who claim they work more than forty to fifty hours per week are usually exaggerating. Plus our mental sharpness and effectiveness severely decline after too many hours working.

APPROACH BUSINESS DECISIONS DISPASSIONATELY

Entrepreneurs bring passion to their work, and that passion fuels their ideas and inspires others. It can also be a double-edged sword, causing you to remain in less-than-favorable situations as your company scales. At some point, most entrepreneurs find themselves with the long-term employee—employee number eight—who's no longer a good fit, who didn't grow their skillset as the company grew. You feel guilty and displeased at having to let this person go; set your own emotions aside for a moment and consider the employee is likely just as unhappy as you are. These decisions are hard, yet necessary.

Delayed tough decisions can create grave repercussions. For example, I invested in a company and they quickly bought another company, but the executives refused to make the difficult decisions required to consolidate roles. They were afraid morale would decline if they let people go. Within nine months, the whole company shut down because the revenue couldn't pay for the extra burden.

Avoiding a tough decision is still a decision. When facing tough decisions, think about the people in your company and the impact your lack of decision may have. Be empathetic toward your employees, but don't let your emotions rule your business sense.

SELF-CARE OF YOU IS SELF-CARE OF THE BUSINESS

Most of us are juggling business, family, and social obligations, not to mention our own need for downtime. You should not be afraid to step back and make sure you've structured your company in a way that prioritizes family, health, and well-being. Anna, the CEO of a large paper manufacturer, structures her work schedule by taking time midday for family and healthcare, then she completes her workday from her home office.

If your personal relationships are falling to pieces because you're not there to invest in them, neither working hard nor trying to recover by playing hard will be helpful. Changes toward self-care need to be prioritized and built into your schedule.

LIFE HACKS

Self-care should be a conversation you have with prospective board members. Not only will you get a feel for their understanding in this area, but they will likely reveal their own best hacks for staying sane in their business and personal lives. I'm familiar with one colleague who eats the same lunch every day, from the same restaurant, because this ensures that he will have one great, healthy meal a day.

Personally, I recommend incorporating necessary family and friend relationships into your work schedule. I call it a hack because you make it part of your workday, like any other business meeting or obligation. You might arrange a meeting downtown to have lunch with your college-age child; a doctor's appointment might be scheduled first thing in the morning on a work-from-home day so the day is not interrupted further. You probably started your company to have more control over your life, so exercise that privilege. As you endeavor to meet the responsibilities of both the business and personal sides of life, seek board members who can be flexible when necessary.

A colleague and I both follow the same philosophy about having our "go-to" outfits. For my regular business days, it's plain black pants and a gray sweater. For public speaking engagements, especially ones with photography or video, I have a red dress and a black jacket. It takes away a whole layer of decisions you need to make. People who adopt this strategy tout the benefits of avoiding "decision fatigue," and it is a great way to start your day quickly and easily.

That same colleague and I also believe in outsourcing whatever is practical. Housecleaning is definitely one of those things. If you think about how valuable your time is plus how stressful a messy house is (I find it stressful, at least), then that service is well worth it. I am also careful to pay my housecleaner well, because I value that work, and if I pay well, I am less likely to experience turnover, which saves me time.

Use a tool like Text Expander or zbook. For frequently used emails or phrases or intros, you can create a short code like "conf" that automatically dumps a standard message about your upcoming conference with links into any platform—social media, document, or spreadsheet. Speed up communications instead of typing the same thing over and over.

THE VALUE OF A GOOD ASSISTANT

Most successful advisors will openly admit that even with productivity tools and time management apps, it's their personal assistant who actually keeps them on track. My assistant proactively plans my day to create pockets of down time. She is aware of which meetings are intense and which meetings are casual, and she avoids scheduling too many high stressors back-to-back. Sometimes I will see a deliberate spacer in my day labeled "for sanity," and I'm grateful for her discernment.

This invaluable member of your team works with you to juggle all that is on your plate. If you struggle to manage your time and you do not employ a personal assistant, I highly recommend that you do so as soon as possible. Some companies hire a "chief of staff" who serves to manage the workflow of the leadership team. It's a similar role, but less focused on personal support.

BEWARE OF BURNOUT

For those who are ambitious and high energy, trying to take time for yourself or slow the pace down is a real challenge, but burnout is a real consequence of overextending yourself. When it occurs, the talents you rely upon to "get it done" lose their sharpness and effectiveness. I've seen entrepreneurs miss key milestones and opportunities because they are too exhausted to take on more. This is the most regrettable kind of business loss, and it's completely avoidable.

* * *

Each entrepreneur's journey to finding their board of directors will be different, but it will likely involve some variation of this timeline:

1. You'll understand that you want to expand;
2. You'll identify areas in which you'd like to deepen your knowledge;
3. The realization of what a board can do for you will strike;
4. You'll carefully calculate the skills you need;
5. Pursuit of board members with those skillsets will begin.

It's customarily an exhilarating time as a business grows to the point of needing a board of directors. It's a symbol of success, the evolution of your business. The decision to move your business forward will ultimately entail some reflection and strategic pursuit of individuals who can help you. To move forward, however, you must first honestly assess your gaps and superpowers. When you identify your knowledge biases, you can then invite people with different perspectives and more experience to your board.

Let's begin with the first step of ANCHOR: Assess.

ACTION STEP: THINK ABOUT YOUR BUSINESS JOURNEY

Part I

Take a few moments to answer these questions as honestly as you can. Feel free to expand your answers in a notebook you can refer back to.

- Where are you on your business journey?
  - Starting out?
  - Growing fast?
  - Taking or seeking investment?
  - Pausing at an inflection point?
  - Thinking about exiting?
- Do you have the product/service and a solid business model?
- What key networks or knowledge do you need to add to your business?

If you can answer these questions, it's time for you to begin the work of building a board of directors.

Part II

In the next chapter, we'll look at the types of people and experience that would best serve your board. In preparation for that chapter, think about the following questions:

- What are the strengths of your company? How do you know?
- What are the weaknesses of your company? How do you know?
- Who are your customers? Who is your biggest customer? Who is your most profitable customer? Do you know?
- What is your business doing today that it wasn't doing two years ago? What are you doing today that you might not be doing in two years?
- Who is your biggest competitor? What do they do well?
- How diversified are your revenue streams?
  - Do you have recurring revenue from your customers (regular revenue that doesn't require pursuing new customers) or are your transactions more "one off"?
  - Do you have contracts with your customers?
  - What is your customer base? Is any one customer more than 15 percent of your revenue?
- What are new markets or customer bases you would be interested in pursuing?

Chapter 2

ASSESS

As a CEO, there are many areas of your business for which you might need advising. Where do you begin? Much like you strategize for your business, you want to strategize for the board, and in today's climate, that means looking to your personal and business values. With a mind toward the values by which you guide your company, you can seek board members whose core values align with yours.

For example, your ideas for company growth may never run low, but finances certainly might. How would you pay a staff, rent an office, and compensate the board? If that's your situation, you need someone with deep, practical knowledge about finances to ensure that you have enough resources to explore ideas for company expansion. And, perhaps you would want that person to value frugality or low risk.

Right along with financials, like the CEOs of many companies, you may have concerns over benefits and salary for new hires, especially if you're competing against large, well-funded companies. It is common for a board of directors to address an organization's budget, and they often home in on employee salaries as the largest expense. If equitable pay is a core value of your business, you want board members who understand your desire to compensate fairly, but you also want to balance your views by more conservative financial viewpoints. (We'll talk about board diversity later in this chapter.)

Work-life integration may be high on your list of values, especially if you or your employees fulfill caregiving roles for family or community. You'd want board members who value and support flexibility to attend to family obligations. A CEO I'll call Kim led her company's board and then experienced a complicated pregnancy. Part of their board agenda included a detailed plan for how to address her impending leave of absence. When her inevitable bedrest was prescribed, the chief operating officer was prepared and stepped into the CEO's role for a few months. You may seek board members who offer that kind of support and are ready to spring into action, if needed. Your colleagues would also need to be connected into the process for these plans to succeed.

In addition to values, you may have specific knowledge or skills gaps that you'd like a board member to fill.

One of the unexpected challenges new CEOs often face is

understanding the amount of taxes, regulations, and legal matters involved in running a company. The last thing you want to happen is to fall short on a compliance issue and have a competitor discredit your work. You want someone on your board who knows how to navigate compliance issues as your company grows.

If your time is consumed with executive affairs, you may need a subject-matter expert to maintain intelligence in the ever-evolving area of quality control and assurance in your focus industries. Not only will you and your staff need regular updates, but as a growing business, you'll need a rearguard protecting the company's systems and processes.

To be clear, a board of directors focuses the collective wisdom of a half dozen or so professionals directly into the company. This can bring you to the next level by helping you to identify new markets, customers, revenue sources or other kinds of business opportunities.

WHAT'S YOUR SUPERPOWER?

I have the ability to look at complex financial data and translate it into something actionable and meaningful—instead of X-ray vision I have XLS-vision. At a glance, I can see a customer that costs too much money or a division that's not profitable. It surprises me when others can't see the numbers that I can see.

Most people underestimate their superpower, because a superpower is typically an innate or learned skill that comes easy to us but is hard for others. I know CEOs who can evaluate the regulatory landscape for opportunities. When I look at how to get from Point A to Point B, I see a crowded wood overgrown with thickets, while they see a complex, yet clear, pathway.

Your company will be most productive when you spend most of your time wielding your superpower. To do so, you must first identify it. You might be surprised at the number and types of talents that could be considered superpowers. Do you see yourself in any of the following?

- Maybe you can walk into a room not knowing anyone and have an interesting conversation with a stranger.
- You might be a visionary who sees a way to completely overhaul operational efficiency.
- Your innate empathy and active listening skills may make you an outstanding personnel manager.
- Seeing and solving the client's problem may mean you are a top notch salesperson or customer service advocate.
- You may have been captain of all the teams in school and continue to be an excellent team builder today.
- You might remember the names and biographical information for hundreds or more people. Successful salespeople and politicians usually have this skill.

We often give superpowers names like:

- organization
- leadership abilities
- fearlessness
- determination

...in other words, there are an endless variety of talents, skills, and strengths.

As CEO, you want to focus your efforts on tasks that take advantage of your strengths and delegate everything else.

When a CEO begins to look at strategically gathering board members who will be most effective in guiding the company, they should first assess their own strengths, limitations, lack of awareness, likes, and dislikes. Creating the best board depends on knowing ourselves and then seeking diverse viewpoints and skills that fill the gaps where we lack ability or interest.

The first step of the ANCHOR process is Assess, which encompasses the following:

- assessing your strengths, skills, talents, aka your superpowers
- assessing your weaknesses, knowledge gaps, and dislikes
- assessing areas where you lack awareness
- assessing where your company is on its growth plan
- assessing your team and the kinds of people you have worked well with in the past—and who are challenging people to work with

Before you hire staff or look for board members, make two lists: one for your superpowers and one for your weaknesses, knowledge gaps, and dislikes. Then, set out to intentionally hire quality individuals to assume the responsibilities associated with the second list. Maybe you don't want to review the profit and loss statements, you don't enjoy creating social media postings, or you don't like dealing with accounts receivable. Don't. Hire qualified personnel to attend to those tasks, and continue applying your superpower to your executive role.

If you are the kind of person who would rather have a small meeting with a couple of key suppliers than go to a big conference, then the suggestion that you become the keynote speaker at the next tech conference isn't going to work for you. That's perfectly acceptable. Seek out an individual with these skills to perform that task within the company. If you don't hire for these positions, you'll be stuck doing the basics of pulling together the company and the services you're offering while you should be focused on the future.

A few years ago, my business partner and I made some hiring and personnel changes, and she turned to me toward the end and said, "I never want to manage a team. I dislike this." I was a bit surprised at first, but as we discussed it, we realized that she'd never had to make such decisions. She had always been the subject-matter expert, so she'd never had to build teams. On the other hand, I had run several teams.

Don't get caught in the weeds; stick to your superpower, and delegate the rest. Of course, this means you must hire people who are different from you, and that applies to the board as well.

THE BENEFITS OF A DIVERSE BOARD

Before forming a consulting firm with a colleague, Lynn was an engineer who specialized in quality control and assurance for a large manufacturer. She and her colleague were able to secure a contract with their former employer as their first customer, and as the years went on, they added more clients to their roster. They hired several people and were making over $1 million annually after a few short years.

When Lynn talked with her clients, she knew there were more opportunities for her, but she wasn't sure how to tackle them. When she went to networking events, she got bits and pieces of advice for how to scale the business, but she didn't know how to pull it all together and prioritize. Lynn knew in theory that it's always easier and better to get more revenue from your existing customers—to land and expand—than to attain new customers; in practice, she was unsure how to implement such a strategy.

Fortunately, Lynn had served on a nonprofit board before. As she sought answers and advice, she quickly realized this endeavor would best be governed by a board of directors. During her term as a board member, she had seen the nonprofit navigate through many challenges. The nonprofit board comprised a range of experiences and personalities, and Lynn felt this diversity of thought and experience made the board effective.

Lynn was most impressed by the strong arguments made by the other board members and staff, and together they came up with a more balanced plan that achieved growth yet retained stability. It was an eye-opening transition to witness, and Lynn knew she wanted that dynamic for the board of her company. To get it, she understood that choosing those with different perspectives would bring about the most engaging and productive discussion. The first three board members Lynn brought on were: a corporate attorney to help guide

her in legal and compliance issues as well as hone her negotiation skills; a former international competitor to serve as a
subject-matter expert and share insights into the changing
marketplace; and the chief financial officer of a large management consultancy to advise on financial strategy.

Creating a board of directors with diverse people, personalities, and skills may seem counterintuitive. We often (wrongly)
assume that like-minded people will get along best and be
most productive. A 2016 article by Harvard Business Review[1]
reports scientific proof that diverse teams bring more innovation and creativity than any one individual, no matter how
educated they are. Think of the board of directors as a team, a
diverse team, that solves problems innovatively and effectively.

A VARIETY OF PERSONALITIES

A balance of various personality types and skillsets creates
the most well-rounded board. To accomplish that goal, you
as CEO must be highly self-aware and honest about your
background and skills. You also want to consider the kinds
of people you prefer dealing with, then deliberately seek out
those with differing perspectives and personalities. The goal
is to create a group of people who think differently than you,
not to create disagreement but to achieve full 360-degree
vision. You want to bring insight to your areas where you have
less awareness, and you achieve that by bringing in people of

---

1   David Rock, Heidi Grant, and Jaqui Grey, "Diverse Teams Feel
     Less Comfortable—And That's Why They Perform Better," Harvard
     Business Review, September 22, 2016, https://hbr.org/2016/09/
     diverse-teams-feel-less-comfortable-and-thats-why-they-perform-better.

different genders, from different cultures or economic backgrounds, different industries and experience.

Let's say Aisha, the CEO of Tech-company A, is a high-energy visionary. When she interviews candidates for the various positions on the board, she rejects the more pensive candidates and chooses those with energy similar to her own. The result of this might be board meetings full of excitement, vision, and potential, but it may be difficult to come to consensus if there are too many visionaries and not enough focus on execution and planning.

Janet, the CEO for Tech-company B, on the other hand, is a cautious, pensive professional. She makes few moves without sufficiently thinking through all of the consequences and possibilities. If this CEO chose board members as cautious as she is, it's not difficult to guess how the board meetings would proceed. Likely, they would be structured, calm, and orderly, but the company might never move forward at the rate tech companies should.

Look for a balance of styles. Who is introverted, and who is extroverted? Who is quick-thinking, and who will ponder the issues? Who will take leadership roles as opposed to those who are better at supportive roles? Both CEOs would benefit greatly from mixing their boards up to include complementary attitudes, points of view, experience, and personalities. Somebody who ponders the issues, like Janet from Company B, would benefit greatly from having at least one board member with quick-decision skills, like Aisha from Company A.

Even though you may be aware that you need skills to balance the gaps in your company, like all of us, you may be inclined to work with those who agree with you. This will produce the exact opposite of a diverse board. Differences bring balance to the board, and it's necessary to pursue your team with this mindset.

FULL REPRESENTATION

To round out your board in a diverse way, think beyond obtaining a marketing expert or chief technology officer, and consider the character, culture, and life experience you are encountering. For CEOs from underrepresented groups such as women, veterans, LGBTQ+, or BIPOC, it is helpful to have some (not all) board members who are from the same underrepresented groups. Diversity counts here too, though; to obtain the most benefit, be careful not to create a monoculture of any one group. As of October of 2021, Nasdaq requires companies that lack women or diverse members on their board to explain why[2]. They've recognized that diverse boards lead to better returns for investors.

CEOs who are new to an industry might look for board members who are more experienced; if they are experienced in their industry, they might consider board members who are not in their industry at all because they need some fresh perspectives.

For example, a CEO for a cancer medical device company has a cardiologist on his board and someone from a pharmaceu-

---

2 Matthew Boyle, "More Corporate Directors Welcome Rules to Increase Board Diversity," Bloomberg, October 12, 2021, https://www.bloomberg.com/news/articles/2021-10-12/ diversity-doesn-t-just-happen-naturally-and-directors-are-finally-realizing-it.

tical company. Each board member provides highly valuable insights from their industries and offers different perspectives than cancer experts would provide.

A CEO who is deeply connected to their community, for example, might look for someone across the country to be on their board; someone who has traveled broadly might consider having a longtime community member on their team.

As CEO, you need to be surrounded by people who will help your company and you as a leader grow and thrive. Having diverse board members who voice diverse opinions will challenge you to think deeply about your ideas, push you to excel, and enable you to accomplish your desired goals. There are many resources to help you manage a diverse board and a diverse team.

Once you understand your superpower and personality traits and consider the traits that might be interesting complements, your board pursuit begins. The next step is to go out and identify board members. Luckily, there are many ways to find your diverse team, and they all revolve around networking.

The following assessment will help you to understand yourself with the goal of finding diverse board members who will complement you. It looks like a lot of questions, but these are things you should be able to answer quickly. As you consider each question, make a goal of seeking board members with different perspectives than your own. As a bonus, this assessment will also help you create a diverse company.

To create a diverse board or even a diverse company, you need to think about all of the different dimensions of diversity. The following questions are a good start in understanding yourself and can be used to learn more about future board members or even for the whole company. As you answer the questions, make a list of the opposite or different trait that would balance your answer; that list will help you form an idea of the types of people you want on your board.

These questions have been administered as part of a Team Diversity Assessment© created by The Impact Seat and used by numerous corporations. (You can also find this assessment at buildyourboardthebook. com.)

When applied to corporate teams, we typically make the survey anonymous and present the data as a composite.

- How many countries have you visited over the course of your life?
- In how many geographic places (regions of a state, states, or countries) have you lived for more than three months in your adult life?
- How many years of college have you had and what kinds of degree(s) do you hold?
- What is your gender identity?

- Identify the paid work you've done that is furthest from the work you do in your current job. (Note that this question is a great icebreaker when getting to know someone.)
- React to this statement: I enjoy a good movie more than a big party.
- React to this statement: I feel a pull toward gregarious people more than standoffish ones.
- How many years have you worked in business?
- How many years have you worked for your company?
- How many languages do you read and speak (with some capability)?
- What is your racial/ethnic identity?
- How many professional events do you typically attend? These can include conferences, workshops, networking events, speaker series, professional association meetings, etc.
- Make a list of as many of those events as you can. If you attend a lot, focus on the past couple of months.
  - Customer events
  - Your own company events
  - Industry or externally organized events
- Do you like going to conferences or networking events?
- Do you have any mental or physical condition that makes it challenging to work (that others may or may not know about)?
- Do you prefer taking in something (book, article, video, etc.) and then proceeding or learning by doing?
- Are you comfortable with not having full information before taking action or do you prefer to have "enough" information before taking action?
- Is your information processing style more parallel or serial?
  - Parallel: I receive information easily from a variety of sources at the same time.
  - Serial: I like to attend to one thing at a time.
- Do you consider yourself more right brained—based in images and

feelings, synthesis—or left brained—based in language, mathematics, categorization?

- Do you characterize yourself as a ponderer or a quick decision-maker?
- Do you characterize yourself as an extrovert—tending to receive energy from spending time with others—or an introvert—tending to receive energy from spending time alone?

Get specific about you, your company, and what you want to accomplish. The following questions help you think more deeply about you, your company, and what you need.

Self-Awareness:

- What do you love most about your job?
- What do you love most about what you're doing?
- What job activity makes you look on your calendar and eagerly anticipate the day?
- What job activity makes you look on your calendar and groan?
- Would you rather go to a conference, or would you rather have a small lunch with a couple industry professionals?
- Are there specific conferences or professional events that you enjoy and specific ones you don't? Why?
- Do you enjoy public speaking?
- Do you enjoy engaging in social media?
- What's the activity you find so fascinating that you get preoccupied with it to the point of forgetting about time?
- What superpowers do you think you need in your business?
- What are your superpowers?
- What would your closest colleagues say are your best skills (or superpowers!)? Ask them!

Chapter 3

NETWORK

Stacy, a successful entrepreneur, found one of her most valued advisors during the creation of her seventh company. She brought extensive business experience and a broad, established network to her new venture, which was in the finance industry, and she needed some long-term advising that was specific to the field. Using the ANCHOR pattern, Stacy first assessed her strengths and weaknesses with regard to the new venture, then asked her network for names of companies similar to hers that were already successful. In one of those companies, she identified a CEO who she thought could advise her. She reached out to introduce herself through a cold email.

Stacy's compelling email led to an in-person meeting. The

CEO expressed interest in Stacy's venture both because of the similarities to his own work and because she wanted to reach an underserved population. When she was visiting his town, she took another bold step and simply asked him to lunch. He accepted, and over time a true rapport developed. He shared valuable insights about the achievements in his business and eventually became the ideal advisor: highly engaged in her industry and vastly supportive. Throughout the year, Stacy kept the lines of communication open by sharing relevant articles and insight for their field. As their trust and rapport grew, the CEO's role evolved from casual advisor to personal mentor. He shared valuable information from his personal experience as an executive, lessons that he learned, and potential damaging situations to be aware of. His generosity with his knowledge and guidance was invaluable to Stacy's success with this particular venture. He's now on the board and has agreed to an advisory role with her company.

NATURAL NETWORKING

The importance of networking cannot be overstated. It is the difference between filling seats and finding your strategic team. As you begin to tap into your network to find board members, understanding the value you bring to the table will help your confidence. You're asking people to be part of something interesting that will be successful. You are also seeking board members who are as excited about the opportunities for your company as you are, who boost your confidence. Don't have the mindset that board members are doing you a favor by being on your board. So many people want to be on boards, because they find it to be interesting work and an opportunity to flex their skills. It will be an interesting and rewarding two-way street.

CEOs also bring new and different ways of looking at existing problems, and most people who serve on boards find that interesting. What's more, those of us on the boards of startups love to have bragging rights when those companies are successful. Whenever CEOs I know are featured on television or in a major publication, I get a vicarious thrill for them!

Millions of legitimate advisors, from all over the world, express interest in board membership. That number may seem exaggerated and yet, at some point in every conversation I have with business professionals, they mention they'd like to serve on a board. These are folks who want to give back to the business community. If you're part of an underrepresented group in corporate America, whether women, Black, Latinx, LGBTQ+, or veterans, there are people who want to help you succeed.

Don't assume these advisors would only be interested in boards of large corporations. The CEO of a smaller company can influence real impact in their field as well as create a dynamic working environment. Entrepreneurs of smaller companies have big professional goals, and board membership provides a chance for an experienced professional to make a difference in the future of their industry. When an entrepreneur I know founded her own company and wanted to form a board of directors, she was incredibly nervous to invite members to the board. She later said, "Today, being so nervous makes no sense, but I was at the time." Many are interested in the experience of advising a fast-growing, more nimble company. Small companies also tend to be innovative, and it's refreshing for an experienced professional to see new ideas in action.

Most companies need advice and expertise in the following categories, and at the beginning of the board pursuit, potential advisors or board members with these skillsets should be on the CEO's radar:

- finance
- marketing
- technology
- human resources/administration
- industry
- risk management

As you network with the intention of finding your board, think about the skills that would fill the gaps at your company. Think about and prepare answers to these questions—we addressed the first two in Chapter 1—as you build a list of people you want to approach:

- What's the giant leap forward for your company?
- What's your next step to get to that milestone?
- Can you reach out to people who have already accomplished this?
- Where can you look to locate them?

As you begin your quest for board members, it's natural to first look within your own immediate circle. Start there, but don't limit yourself to your local network alone. You may need to reach far to find those who can help your company grow exponentially. As I said, people with backgrounds and experience you need are all over the globe, and they want to be board members.

Let's look at the concentric circles of your network and how to approach people in each.

YOUR NETWORK

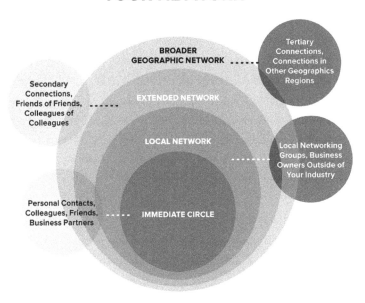

LOCAL AND EXTENDED NETWORKING

As you reach out locally, think about people in your immediate circle. What other business owners do you know, also outside of your industry? Who do you bank with, buy from, sell to? This is your local network, and it likely extends far beyond who you'd typically consider a close friend or business associate.

Now, let's say you consider your inner circle to be five executives in your coworking space or from a local networking group. Who do they know? Who do they bank with, buy from, sell to? That is your extended network. Your board of directors brings their extended network to you. This is why finding board members willing to connect you to those who can help you will expand your business.

When you find prospective board candidates, openly discuss your interest in creating a board of directors. Ask for some specific advice on the subject. You will be surprised at how much knowledge and experience people have. Stick with a polite request that carries no pressure or implied commitment. This type of approach tends to make people feel free to respond candidly, and their honest insight is what you are looking for. Much of the success you'll see in having a board relies on quality relationships being established, so demands or aggressive pursuit will likely backfire.

Be sure to ask about their specific experiences, rather than limiting your questions to their opinions. We all know that people like to give their opinions freely, but you want to learn about the actual experience they have. For example, instead of asking, "What do you think about hiring an HR consultant?" Ask them what experience they have managing their HR. It's a simple re-phrasing that is effective.

Especially when asking for advice about raising capital, start with asking questions about the person's experience. If the person is a casual member of an angel investor group and makes one investment a year, that is a far different situation than someone who manages a small venture fund or raised venture capital themselves.

Most business organizations that you are part of likely have a board of directors already established. Talk to the board chair of these organizations; reach out and ask them what you need to know or what they think about boards of directors in your industry. Ask them to describe their most effective board member, and perhaps ask for an introduction so you can gain insight to the traits of an effective board member. You can seek out any type of advice you feel you need for your board.

Oftentimes, your local organization is part of a national membership, and that could be a path to a broader geographic network. Clearly communicate to your local leadership that you are looking to build a board of directors, and you're open to expanding into different geographies. Ask them if they have connections in other regions. If they're not helpful or you don't want to go that route, there's no reason why you can't reach out to the national organization for that local chapter.

I'm on the board of a company that's based in California, and most of the original board members reside on the West Coast. The geographical distance naturally means I bring new contacts from an entirely different region, namely the East Coast. As business moved forward, I was able to provide the CEO with some East Coast introductions, but beyond that, I was able to convey background information on the market and the regional leaders for the CEO and executive team to make productive connections. The company took off, increasing business in both the West Coast and East Coast markets. That's the magic of expanding your borders. That board now has representatives from across the United States and internationally.

ONLINE NETWORKING

When you've exhausted your local and extended network for potential board members, you can turn to the internet to find prospects. There are also many online business forums on Twitter and other social media platforms, which can usually yield some legitimate potential board members. We're going to focus on LinkedIn as our social-media-of-choice because of their hundreds of millions of members from all over and their commitment to being a business platform.

Most people who have board experience list it on LinkedIn. As you find them, ask yourself if their background is relevant to what you need. What kinds of posts and comments do they leave? Do they seem interesting? Do they show industry acumen? Can you see them assisting in the governance of your company? What would they bring to the table? A more robust following may lead to secondary connections; are they connecting with a vast community, or are they fairly isolated?

Directly searching LinkedIn for the position you are trying to fill is another option. Let's say the CEO owns an insurance company, and she's looking for a social media expert with legitimate marketing credentials. Here's where she uses social media to find people from all different geographical locations that meet her criteria. Decide on a company or customer name who is a big player in your space. Our insurance saleswoman might select Geico Insurance.

She would then enter "chief marketing officer at Geico Insurance" into her search bar. She may not get a direct hit of that individual, but all kinds of folks who do similar work will pop up. Look into the backgrounds of the search results to find prospects: Does their experience look interesting? Is there any indication that they might consider being a board member, such as prior board service, whether for profit or not-for-profit?

It will be helpful to keep good records of your contacts with a note as to why, specifically, that individual is on your radar. In my experience, your memory is not as trustworthy as you may believe. Use a spreadsheet or contact management app to list all of the interesting prospects you've found. Have their names, contact information, and LinkedIn bios clear and available.

Are any of these people connected to you already through your existing network? If so, you can request a warm introduction; if not, you can approach them with a cold email or message.

Board recruiters exist to help CEOs find board candidates. Bigger boards, whether they're for a charity or for public companies, use recruiters to manage that process about 10 percent of the time. These are consultants that help the CEO set up their board, learn best practices for running a board, and in some cases, provide instruction to the prospective board member. Our experience has been that board recruiters usually have a network of prospects that they work with, and these pools typically lack diversity. In addition, board recruiters can be costly.

There are also organizations particularly focused on getting more women on boards. Those organizations focus a lot on training, and they have some connections to get their candidates installed as board members. These types of organizations focus on diversity and offer that as a benefit. You can find these groups by a simple online search of "board training for women."

Training for nonprofit boards is popular, and this can be particularly useful due to the complexity of nonprofit rules. These groups train nonprofit leaders on how to run their board and also train board members. An online search for "nonprofit board training" will yield several results.

WARM INTRODUCTIONS

A warm introduction happens when you and the person you want to meet share a common connection. First, reach out to your shared connection, learn about your targeted contact, and confirm they're a good fit for your goals. Then, figure out the best approach for connecting with them. The level of introduction varies. Some contacts may say you can mention their name in your cold email, and others will go the extra mile and reach out to the shared contact to introduce you directly—that's the best result.

A note about introductions: it is essential to follow the "double opt in" rule for introductions. If you ask me for an introduction to someone I know, I will reach out to that person and see if they are willing to connect. That person can decline, although more often than not they accept. Never connect two people without getting permission from each party. At best, you are inconveniencing someone, at worst you are creating an awkward situation.

COLD OUTREACH

Cold outreach is most successful when your efforts reach your target contact at just the right time, with just the right authentic message. Stacy, the CEO described at the start of this chapter, achieved this brilliantly as she had done her research and understood her "target's" interests and current projects before reaching out.

Many of us cringe at the thought of cold outreach, but at times it may be your only option to meet and access the type of people who can help grow your business. If you're entering a new field or geographic location, cold communication may be the only way to connect with someone beyond your first- and second-level contacts. A well-crafted, personalized email can come close to an in-person (cold) encounter in the absence of a warm introduction. To that end, if you are going to capture your reader, your communication must stand out. Below are examples of good cold communications.

If you don't have the option of getting a warm introduction to someone you've identified as a potential board member, the internet allows you to make your own connections. Googling your prospect is a natural first step because any relevant news and/or business articles about them will be at your disposal. You need that information to craft a compelling email.

A cold email (or a cold phone call) should have a couple of key elements. First, think about why you want to reach out to the person. Are they an industry leader? Do they also own their own business in an adjacent industry? Have you heard about them and think their ideas are interesting? Did you read about them in an article? Is there a specific piece of advice you'd like from them? Make a list of the reasons why you want to talk to them and what you want to learn from them.

Second, make a list of why they would want to talk to you. Many business leaders want to help others succeed, but that may not be enough to entice someone to respond to your request. However, don't underestimate how flattering it is for someone to reach out for expertise.

Third, figure out how to reach out to the person. I prefer using LinkedIn because it allows the person I am messaging to see my background and (hopefully) some connections we may have in common. I sent some cold messages on LinkedIn when conducting research for this book. I usually referenced how I heard about the person and said I'd like to have a conversation with them about their own board of director experiences.

Finally, keep it short. You don't need to tell them your life history; simply write, "I am the CEO of XYZ company in ABC industry. I am curious how you [insert something noteworthy]." You could even see in their profile if they are on boards of directors themselves and ask for advice on how to build a board in your industry.

Today there are many CRM (customer relationship management) software tools that allow you to automate emails and then send updates based on whether they opened the email. I do not recommend an automated process; a personal touch is essential. You are not trying to get a thousand new customers; you are trying to add three to five people to your board. On average, you'll talk to ten to twenty people to accomplish this.

SCRIPTS FOR COLD EMAIL OR CALLS

Whether it's a phone call and email or a LinkedIn message, you want to make your message as personalized as possible. Follow this simple three-step format:

- Who you are—keep it short. "I'm CEO of a financial consulting firm. I've been in business for four years and am looking to expand my network of advisors with the plan to build a board of directors."
- Why you noticed them. "I see on LinkedIn that you are a marketing executive at Company XYZ. I read your recent blog post on new trends, and I would like to ask your advice on some new business I am considering."
- What you'd like as a next step. "I am planning to attend the ABC conference. Are you attending? We could meet up. If not, I'd love to chat via Zoom. Can we schedule something for the week of X?"

MEETING BOARD CANDIDATES

When the time comes to meet prospective board members, keep this human tendency in mind, and use it to your advantage: people love to talk about themselves. Let them, and when they do, pay close attention to their experience and involvement in their industry. Ask questions about what you saw in their bio. Be prepared with questions about their company involvement, experience, and achievements.

Since discussion will naturally progress toward the company, you should have your priorities for this current year top of mind: plans that you're working on and strategic considerations should be ready for discussion. It is somewhat of an interview process, so project confidence as you convey a desire to get to know your prospects.

As you have conversations with individual candidates, take detailed notes in your list, and keep this information together so you can quickly access it. As your list grows, you will be thankful that you developed a system of checking off who you've made contact with and how the interaction went.

FAMILY BUSINESS PARTNERS

Family businesses have their own unique dynamic. There are countless successful family-run businesses, and they tend to have a couple of common traits:

- an understanding of the specific roles each family member plays
- constant communication among the members

It's interesting to note these traits are critical to a successful board of directors as well.

In the investing world, most investors will not invest in companies where the leadership team is related. The power dynamic among family members is typically strong, and some investors believe it's an obstacle to hiring top talent, because they cannot compete with the family dynamic.

I don't have that bias. I evaluate the situation on a case-by-case basis. In many cases, family businesses have highly talented people in roles that are hard to fill. I've seen companies with top-notch CFOs, CTOs, and other positions filled by family members, while comparable companies could not recruit that level of talent.

But the dynamic needs to be acknowledged. Having a family-dominated board of directors could be challenging if the operations are also family dominated. I recommend that family businesses use the board of directors to get outside expertise and perspective. Engage in a deep analysis of the family members' skills and expertise and especially their working style, then build a complementary board that brings diversity to the company.

FRIEND DON'T LET FRIENDS SERVE ON THEIR BOARDS

A final caveat when thinking about who will best serve the board of your company: avoid your personal friends. It may bolster your confidence to have a friendly face on the board, but you will not get the support you need and could jeopardize your friendship. Keep good friends as advisors and get independent experts on your board. Besides, who can you complain to if your good friend is on the board?

ADVISORS

As you network, you'll likely identify many candidates who seem appropriate for your board. Asking them to take on an advisory role for a few months before approaching them to join the board allows you both to test the waters and make sure it's a good fit. If you've made a good connection with someone, try to maintain it. Offer to stay in touch. Ask them if they would be open to providing the occasional word of advice. Often, you will get a positive response for this type of continued communication. If your prospective candidate is open to this, be sure to follow up and keep those lines open.

MEMBERS OF THE BOARD

A board of directors is not only the secret sauce to growing your company, but also the foundation upon which you can build a solid company that is resilient in the face of challenges and successful in achieving its goals. In this section we will outline some of the legal and structural elements of your board of directors.

BOARD CHAIR

A successful serial entrepreneur I know in the tech industry relayed a story about approaching the person who eventually became her board chair. She first met him as the seventh employee at his social media startup. Impressed with his business acumen, she took notes on every move he made. Later when she was forming the board for the company she founded, she asked him to be the chair. She told me, "I never thought twice about having someone else fill the board chair position. I look at it like a coach." He was excited to accept the position and took it very seriously. When they procured substantial funding, it was a group victory for her and board members alike.

The most foundational element for your board is a strong board chairperson. While many CEOs also carry the title of Chairperson of the Board, I advise against that choice for several reasons:

- Many CEOs are first-time business leaders and have limited executive experience. There is already a lot of learning in the CEO role, which means there's no bandwidth to also learn to be a board chair.
- If a CEO is also trying to run the board, then they are not running their company.
- Many CEOs have never served on a board, let alone been a chair, and the health of the company will be made vulnerable by a CEO learning on the job.
- Even experienced CEOs know that the split of duties between a CEO and a board chair makes holding the dual role untenable.

So why do so many CEOs want to run their board? One simple answer: control. They believe that controlling both positions gives them greater control over the company, and they especially want to prevent their own ouster. A board of directors can, if given the right powers, fire the CEO. Later on in this book, we will describe how to possibly avoid this problem or at least manage and reduce the risk.

Being replaced as CEO, especially for a company you founded, can be an awful experience, but with the right structures in place you can minimize that risk. Also, if your company is successful, you are less likely to be replaced.

Then again, every CEO should think about whether or not some day they want to continue to run their company. A board of directors is an excellent resource for thinking through the future of the company.

Key characteristics of a board chair include:

1. Prior board experience. If they've never chaired before, they certainly can step into the role, but without previously having participated on several boards, it will be difficult to manage the role effectively.
2. A close working relationship with the CEO. They don't have to be best friends, but the chair and the CEO need to have a professional working relationship with open communication.
3. Communication and organizational abilities to connect with the rest of the board of directors and manage politics and personalities.
4. A healthy respect for procedure to ensure votes are properly taken and good governance is followed.
5. An understanding of the big picture for the company and the willingness to use their social capital when needed.
6. A network or the ability to grow their own network to identify additional effective board members.

SECRETARY AND TREASURER

Certain board roles are often legally required, two of which are a secretary and a treasurer. As with all legal matters, check with your attorney about the rules for the jurisdiction you operate and are incorporated in. Generally, the secretary of the board keeps the minutes of the meeting, particularly documenting board votes. The position is typically held by a board member, but I've been on many boards where the company's lawyer attends the meeting, oftentimes free of charge or as part of their overall retainer fee, and they make sure that the notes are properly prepared. Consult with your attorney regarding rules for your particular circumstances.

The board meeting minutes are not a transcription of the meeting, but rather a summary of action items and votes taken. It is typically not onerous.

The treasurer doesn't work in the company or have access to company finances; they report on the financial condition of the company. The treasurer usually remains distant from any type of audit and finance committee so that they can identify situations such as control processes and risks. Here, too, you'll want to obtain all rules and regulations regarding your treasurer from your attorney, and it may be helpful to include your CPA as an advisor to the situation as well.

INVESTORS AND REPRESENTATIVES

Investors, particularly venture capitalists, often expect to have a seat on the board of directors so they can monitor their investment and provide guidance and influence.

As an investor, I have taken board seats because I want to ensure my interests are represented. However, it is important to note that when you serve on the board of directors, you have a responsibility to make decisions for the benefit of the company and not specific investors. In lieu of a board seat, however, I often prefer an "observer" seat which provides me with access to the board discussions without the obligation of a full board member. I also do not have a vote on matters, and the board can meet without observers present.

In a typical venture capital investment, the lead investor will take a board seat, typically representing all the investors in that particular round of investment. The structure of the board is a standard part of a fundraising negotiation with a lead investor.

Investors are important contributors to your board of directors, and you want to make sure that you have some control and input into who takes that position. In later stage venture capital investments, it is typically the partner from the investment fund who leads the fundraising round who takes the board seat. This is the natural progression in forming a close working relationship with one of the most influential people for your company.

In other cases, companies may have no investors, or they only have small, passive investors, or maybe there are investors who are prohibited from taking a board seat. In that case, you may have more flexibility in the type of board you construct.

INDEPENDENT BOARD SEAT

As a company grows and a board expands, it adds what's called an "Independent Board Seat" (or several), which is explicitly designed to have a voice on a board of directors that is independent from any ownership or company leadership. These folks are usually experienced board members who are subject matter or market experts in the field.

Step by step, you will fill the seats on your board. Proper, intentional communication from the beginning lays the foundation for a successful board. Let's look at the C in ANCHOR, Communication.

ACTION STEP: CONTACT YOUR NETWORK

- Write your introductory letter.
- Find at least one local contact and at least one long-distance contact, and write an introductory letter to each.
- Adjust your letter to what you find in your research about the person. Remember to be concise; get to the point directly.
- Track your progress with either an organizational app or notebook.

Chapter 4

COMMUNICATE

So far, we've focused on why you need a board, the types of people who can best help you, and how to find them. Once you've gotten your team together, it's time to begin addressing the issues in your company and scaling your business. How do you bring this group into your company processes and begin reaping the benefits of your board of directors?

ONBOARDING

It may take months to identify your first couple of board members, and when you have those first two or three members, you will need to be prepared to onboard them. Onboarding means spending time with each board member individually, then collectively discussing your company and vision. Onboarding a small group is easier than one person at a time, because it is almost the same amount of work to onboard one person as it is three. You have to prepare the most recent information, provide background information, and make introductions to key people. Some boards have "classes" where they add a couple of board members at a time.

Larger, high-profile boards may have a more formal onboarding process, but keeping operations somewhat informal often works most effectively for small boards and smaller companies. Provide the board members with a packet of information about the company. Include some history, and provide organizational charts, bios of the top executives at the company, your own bio, and specific areas of interest to you, as the CEO. A thorough and well-thought-out profile of each board member should be developed and shared with the group as well.

Aim to understand each board member's most relevant experience. We tend to focus on a person's most recent experience, but sometimes it's their knowledge from years ago that becomes most applicable. For example, I personally have served on a board where there was fraud at the organization. It was a valuable experience that took place years before and would not necessarily be listed on my LinkedIn profile. As a result of that experience, I learned to "trust, but verify," a philosophy that has successfully guided my interests since. It has also made me laser focused on financial and accounting procedures and policies to minimize risk.

Having your board meet and begin to connect is the first step to building the rapport needed for success. Camaraderie is vital among those who will be governing the company, and you should set the tone for this atmosphere through your verbal and written communication.

ESSENTIAL COMMUNICATION

I sit on the board of a company that currently has several acquisition offers on the table. They are right in the middle of negotiating their next steps. The CEO has been regularly feeding us, the board members, information throughout this process. Recently, she called a special board meeting to get everybody on the same page, and since we'd been paying attention and getting information all along, we had a highly constructive conversation.

Compare that with a board meeting where the main topic was staffing and hires, and the strategy to move forward was detailed and complex. We were presented with the information *at the board meeting*, with no time to process it. Many of the board members had negative reactions to the types of people that were going to be hired, the pay that they were going to get, and movements within the company. We wasted a lot of time without resolving the issues because we didn't have time to process this intricate data.

Staying in communication with your board is the secret sauce to its success. Frequent conversations with your board members allow them to listen to your concerns and give you feedback. When everyone comes together under those conditions, as in our first example above, there's already consensus to some extent. There are at least no surprises.

BENEFITS OF TRANSPARENT COMMUNICATION

Transparent communication oftentimes shines light on board members' broader skills and knowledge that you might have been unaware of. The most interesting innovations come from a collaboration of diverse skills and experience.

You want to create an atmosphere that encourages board members to share their experience beyond their specific position. For example, you may lean on a board member with HR experience for advice about hiring and firing, however, most of your board members probably have some experience with those tasks as well—experience that may be directly applicable to your situation. If the HR board member comes from a corporate enterprise but you need to fill technical roles within your startup, their experience may be less valuable than the entrepreneur who has launched multiple tech companies. Encouraging board members to share about their broad experience helps you identify the best. You may be genuinely surprised by the valuable contributions you receive from board members who do not have direct expertise on the subject matter.

DEALING WITH PERSONALITIES

Central to your success in getting the most out of the personality types you've assembled is understanding why they are necessary and respecting what they bring to the table. If you've assembled a diverse board in terms of gender, race, and experience, the members are likely diverse in their communication and personality styles as well. The best way I've found to address varying personality and communication styles is *to prepare all board materials in advance.*

Early preparation and delivery of board materials is the gateway to handling diverse personalities. Each member will handle advanced materials differently, and providing ample time to review the information in advance allows each member to process the data in their own way. Your quick thinkers may not read them until the morning of your quarterly meeting. Your ponderers, however, will be able to provide their best opinion after processing the documents. During this time, make yourself available to them should they have any questions, because the ponderers likely will.

During board gatherings, don't let any one person dominate the conversation. Extroverts will naturally do this if they are left unchecked, and you will not have the best outcome in that scenario. The goal of having your diverse team, again, is to hear the perspectives of all of the people on your board. Given the time to make their conclusions without the interference of quick-decision teammates, I've seen the ponderer personality types come up with fantastic ideas and solutions.

PROTECT YOUR MATERIALS

There was a time, not long ago, when meeting together as a board meant materials were handed out and then collected at the end of the meeting so that no information left the room. In our new digital workplaces, however, that seems to be less common of an occurrence. We live in an electronic era, and we're looking for diverse board members who could be based all over the globe. In this scenario, a quality board meeting may have to take place by videoconference. In all cases, the company needs to consider how to keep sensitive information confidential.

Many of the cloud services we all use do not have the security you need.

When sharing information, be cautious about how you send it. I recommend using a secure portal to share documents. This portal can control what information is allowed to be viewed, printed, or downloaded. Many of them also include a water-mark for each document downloaded so you know where information came from if you discover it "out in the wild." You can also turn access on and off in a matter of moments as the administrator. Some video conferencing technologies also block screenshots, but of course a cell phone aimed at the screen can capture the image, albeit not as well.

Having a digital repository for materials is also helpful when onboarding new board members. You can easily provide new members with the appropriate historical context and back-ground information.

Companies usually take great measures to keep financial information, HR details, and high-level matters private. It is essential to be clear with your board about what information is particularly confidential. Some issues are sensitive, but it may be unclear if they are strictly confidential. For instance, companies sometimes keep client names confidential, and other times they publicize their top clients. It will be up to the CEO to consciously and consistently communicate which matters need to be kept confidential.

MEETING CADENCE

One CEO I work with schedules a one-on-one call between us every week, same time, same day. To prep for that call, she usually sends a short email highlighting the topics she'd like to cover. There might be something I need to do, such as review a financial report before the call, and this will be outlined in the email. Other board members may only speak with her on a biweekly or monthly schedule.

Time is always a big concern when dealing with busy, in-demand professionals, so scheduling regular calls, well in advance, is best. In fact, your board schedule for the next twelve months should be prepared and distributed as soon as possible so your board members can get back to you with any conflicts. As long as you are communicating on a weekly or monthly basis with your board members individually, there should be no one that you haven't talked to from one board meeting to the next. Ideally, you want to strive for a schedule similar to this:

- Quarterly board meeting: This is in-person, not a video-conference, if at all possible. In-person communication brings an intangible element of getting to know one another, so insist on maintaining the in-person gathering.
- Monthly: This can be an email or maybe a quick videoconference or recording. Monthly updates keep each board member up to date on company progress.
- Weekly: Informally, on a weekly or biweekly basis, check in with each member of the board by phone. This frequent, less formal communication lays the best foundation.

This schedule should be combined with some social events such as dinner before or after the board meeting. You're looking to build comradery among those who govern your company. Like any other team-building situation, those on your board should feel comfortable and able to work well with each other.

One CEO gasped when I suggested this cadence. At the time, she was overwhelmed by a large amount of reporting due, and I explained that if we check in every Friday, no news will be startling because we'll regularly discuss what's on the horizon. We now have regular quarterly board meetings, and she has a weekly call with almost every board member. These calls do not have to be hours long; limiting your calls to thirty minutes can accomplish a lot.

THE WEEKLY CALL

Many entrepreneurs feel that communication between board meetings can be sufficiently handled by email, or worse, by newsletter. I strongly advise against this. First of all, in the typical tsunami of an inbox that busy people are dealing with, there's a high risk they'll miss the message. Don't substitute regular communication with your board with a newsletter or email-type report. Talk to your board members, by phone or in person, at least voice-to-voice, if not face-to-face.

If you think of board meetings as major landmarks, then the weekly calls are the roads that lead there. People are more honest and forthcoming in a private phone conversation than in a group setting. Their instant response typically cannot be concealed, and you can have a direct dialogue around an issue.

If you think you don't have enough to talk to them about every week, you'll be surprised at how much comes up and gets accomplished during a low-pressure, weekly check-in with a board member. Particularly if you have a company that is growing fast, the weekly call—or biweekly call, depending on your need to communicate with that board member—will not only keep each board member abreast of company growth and change, but also will build the necessary rapport between you and each board member.

Every CEO I have worked with tells me things over the phone that they would never put in an email, let alone a newsletter. I have helped counsel a CEO over a decision to replace an executive, how to manage a difficult customer, cash flow problems, and many, many other sensitive issues. This informs me, as a board member, of real-time situations so that I am rarely surprised by news from outside sources.

Speaking frequently allows me to take small actions such as connecting the CEO with a contact or sending information to them on an issue we have discussed beforehand. If we were only connecting on a monthly basis, I would not have as deep a connection with the company. I also feel like when I connect with a CEO frequently, I actually spend less time on the company because I am up to speed on the day-to-day business and am more effective in offering advice and guidance.

There is a presumption that instead of actually speaking by phone on a weekly basis, a board meeting will run smoothly if you simply prepare a good presentation or board package. This has proven to be false over and over again. The presentation should be prepared, but by the time your board sees it, they should be well aware of the information that is in it because you have been speaking to them weekly or biweekly about the topics and sending materials to review before the board meetings. This being the case, that presentation is not going to be an hour-long presentation, but a short list of highlights to cover.

FREQUENCY

When do we meet? When do we call? When do we email? If you have regularly scheduled phone calls and board meetings with your board members, the only time you would veer from that structure would be if you need a rapid response for something. Other than that, stick to that weekly or biweekly phone call, and try to accomplish as much as possible during that time.

Email should be used for things that require a documented response or for sending reports and useful research materials. In an email, outline your expectations for the feedback or action you would like from the recipient.

On a practical level, this communication prepares the board well. Human nature is designed to look for risks and problems when things are sprung on them. Generally, people prefer to have some advance notice and be able to process a situation. When plans are presented without giving prior warning, CEOs run the risk of the board replying protectively, focusing on hazards and negatives.

Perceptive CEOs quickly discover that good business relationships are at the heart of their board. Good communication is the most important tool used to build and maintain those good relationships. Good relationships also lean on following best legal practices, which is the next letter of ANCHOR, Honor Legal Duty.

**ACTION STEP: SET UP YOUR
CALENDAR AND CADENCE**

- Develop and communicate the schedule for regular board meetings.
- Block time on your calendar for individual weekly or biweekly calls.

Chapter 5

HONOR LEGAL DUTY

Most of my investments are in high-growth tech companies that raise venture capital to scale quickly. The startup culture of Silicon Valley has heavily influenced the mindset around boards of directors of these companies. Most venture capitalists in Silicon Valley want to keep boards of directors small, so that there are fewer voices around the table. I am strongly opposed to small boards of directors. It doesn't mean I won't participate—I certainly have served on small boards—but I think larger boards, and the diversity they can offer, are more effective.

The typical trajectory is that most startups begin with the CEO and perhaps another founder as the sole members of the board. With each fundraising round, a company would then typically add one board member to represent the lead investors. As time goes on, early investor members of the board drop off and the largest, latest investor takes a board seat, probably as the chair of the board. Those board seats and the structure of the board are an important part of the investment negotiation with any kind of venture capital firm or other institutional investor.

Delaying forming a more robust board—with, perhaps, five members—until you have raised a larger venture capital round deprives you and your company of the opportunities to add expertise critical to a startup and to expand your network.

Others may argue that you can achieve the same results with advisors or even a board of advisors. I can tell you from experience, advisors are not as effective as a board of directors. Most advisory boards are not actually boards—they are a series of one-on-one relationships between the CEO and the advisors. It doesn't harness the power of the group, and that is what a board of directors does well.

Work with your attorney to understand and implement the different details of your legal documents to determine what kind of board you can have and if you need to make changes.

The legal structure of your company influences the agreement the company signs with board members. To oversimplify things, there are two basic kinds of legal structures: the corporation, or C Corp; and the formation of a partnership, LLC, or S Corp.

For a corporation, the company is owned by shareholders. In

the case of small businesses, those shareholders may be only one or two people. The shareholder agreement outlines the roles and responsibilities of the board. The company can then have individual agreements with each board member.

In a partnership, there is an operating agreement that states how the partnership is managed, including whether there is a board and what the board can do. Boards are often less explicitly named in partnership agreements.

For many of the readers of this book, your business may have the legal format of an LLC, which is a limited liability company. Those companies are not explicitly structured to have a board of directors, but in my opinion that provides your company with more flexibility. Your board of directors would have fewer legal and fiduciary obligations than a corporation's board would, and you can still benefit from all of the structure and support outlined in this book.

Important: While your attorney is involved in creating board-related documents, it's a great idea to take time to review your corporate documents as well and do any general cleanup necessary.

TERMS AND AGREEMENTS

Equally important as having the right people on the CEO's team is having a legal agreement to protect their interests. Finding a qualified corporate attorney is at the top of the list of things the CEO needs to do to initiate the formation of their board. It's a well-known fact that the cost of a good corporate lawyer deters companies from employing one, but at the end of the day, you pay now or pay later. This thinking can get the CEO into a lot of trouble. It's critical to have a lawyer examine any kind of agreement the CEO is signing, even simple agreements with their vendors. To skip this step when assembling a board can cause legal nightmares for you and your business down the road.

You want to take steps to protect yourself and your business. You need a personal and a corporate attorney to advise you on the following topics:

AVOID GETTING OUSTED

Many entrepreneurs have a real fear of a board taking over their company and ousting them. There are headlines every day about CEOs being ousted. How can a CEO protect themselves while also creating an effective board?

Important decisions are often required to be voted on by the shareholders, and the majority owner controls a lot of the company governance. For many small- and medium-size corporations, this means a CEO who is the majority shareholder can control the company.

However, there are some extreme and egregious cases where

CEOs structured their company to keep control. Mark Zuckerberg, CEO and chair of the board of Facebook's parent company, Meta, has special "voting shares" that give him a disproportionate number of votes compared to other shareholders. Many people have criticized Facebook and how Zuckerberg is not held accountable like other CEOs. Note that Facebook also goes against my other recommendation to not have your chairperson be the CEO. Zuckerberg has learned all his roles "on the job" with little accountability.

Adam Neumann, the former CEO of WeWork, was also able to negotiate special "voting shares" that gave him more voting power despite not owning a majority of the company. His voting power also meant that he needed to be given extra payouts to relinquish control of the company while shareholders, especially employees, saw the value of their stock plummet.

Fortunately, especially for investors, we are not seeing these extreme cases proliferate. A well-known Silicon Valley attorney told me that these structures still exist but they are now much more rare. That doesn't mean that a CEO shouldn't consider legal protection for themselves. Speak with an attorney who specializes in executive compensation. You might be able to get some advice from your corporate attorney; however, your corporate attorney is ethically obligated to protect the rights of the company and not you as the CEO.

PROTECT YOURSELF WITH TERM LIMITS

Boards of directors of large institutions such as universities, hospitals, or publicly traded companies have board members who serve for a decade or more, for good reasons. Those organizations have complex rules for operations, and a steep learning curve exists for board members to be fully effective. A lot of time and investment goes into the board positions, committee leaders, and chair. For larger entities, a ten-year term might make sense as the board member rotates through committees and then takes a chair position on a committee or on the board itself.

Oftentimes in nonprofit organizations, we see long-standing board members. It's common to see a certain staleness about these boards. Large donors with a bent toward prestige often are the holders of those long-term seats. This is not the dynamic and active board I would recommend for entrepreneurs who are seeking to advance.

Many entrepreneurs don't think about term limits when setting up a board.

For small companies, the CEO should have the ability to turn their board over quickly to match the board with the needs and pace of the company. For a fast-growing company, the CEO wants to have the flexibility to keep the board highly engaged in the short term. To this end, the CEO's attorney can include term limits in the legal board agreements. Implementing a three-year term limit, with the option to renew, is a good rule of thumb. This gives the CEO some recourse with those who are not effective.

Be aware, however, that if there are outside investors, they will often negotiate the terms of a board seat that is tied to fundraising. For companies that raise investment, often new rounds of investment mean a new board configuration, but that isn't always ideal.

In the earlier days of a company's growth, a board composed of operators, market experts, and entrepreneurs makes sense. They will help guide the company as it establishes its foundation. You always want to add people to your board who have the experience for where you want to grow next. As the legendary hockey player Wayne Gretzky would say, he skated to where the puck was *going to* be, not to where it already was.

BOARD MEMBER AGREEMENTS

As much as is possible, share the same agreement with all members, but in some circumstances, individual agreements are more appropriate. Perhaps the CEO is compensating some board members and not others. It is not common to compensate board members who are representing investors, but it is common to compensate independent board members. The agreement would include this information, along with the term limit for that person, expectations about their time commitment, and any items specific to their situation. Because of the number of legal agreements that need to be in place, particularly for C Corps, expect to be relying heavily on your corporate attorney during board establishment.

Important: Your corporate attorney is the attorney for the company and not for you personally. Be aware that you may need to obtain separate legal advice from a different kind of lawyer to protect your personal interests.

INSURANCE

All companies with a board of directors should have directors and officers (D&O) insurance. This insurance protects the company's board and officers from being sued for a range of situations, excluding fraud. D&O insurance prevents board members and executives from personal liability involving the company.

Companies should also have "key person" insurance on the CEO. Most investors require this to protect their investment, but it is always a good idea to prevent a company from going out of business if something happens to the CEO.

COMPENSATING YOUR BOARD

In my research for this book, I relied on my own experiences as a board member and that of my colleagues. When I researched the topic of compensation, I found that there was no one answer for how to compensate a board member, regardless of the size of the company or the industry. Keep asking your network what they are seeing with companies similar to yours.

Most board members will receive a small stipend to be on your board, and it will vary with the size and the type of company. Some board members may also get a small amount of equity in your company. And by "small," in some cases, it starts off as 0.25 percent to 0.5 percent. That's a teeny sliver of your company.

If you choose to give a small amount of stock to your board members (or advisors or employees) make sure that this amount vests over time. Typically the vesting period is about three to four years. That prevents you from giving equity to someone who turns out to be a bad fit and leaves the board after a short time.

If you have a board member who is also an investor in the company, they are basically acting as a steward of that investment. Most board members who represent investors do not get extra stock from early stage companies. That changes as a company grows. There can always be exceptions if you judge that person to be deserving of extra compensation.

CONFLICTS OF INTEREST

All companies, and especially boards of directors, should have conflict of interest policies. There are so many ways that companies can have conflicts, and it is important to be transparent and proactive in establishing policies.

Let's say a board member fails to disclose that the candidate they recommended as the CEO's next chief financial officer is a relative; perhaps the chair of a certain board owns the building that the business rents out of; another CEO has a customer on the board who buys services from them. These are types of clear conflicts of interest, and it's vital that a process for addressing conflicts of interest be established with your attorney. Typically, transparency is the best policy.

Another type of conflict of interest lies with the board member's role outside the board. If, for instance, an HR consultant holds a seat on the CEO's board, the CEO should not feel obligated to use their service. If a CEO questions the motives of their advisors, whether they are there to render advice or sell a service, it creates a lack of trust. This sort of situation should be deliberately avoided, and the legal agreement will likely have a place for prospective members to sign off on this type of conflict.

Knowing your legal obligations and honoring your duty to the legal side of establishing a board will help to protect you before problems arise. Another form of protection comes from your own ability to pull your board together and get organized, which is the O of ANCHOR, Organize.

ACTION STEP: MAKE IT LEGAL

- Hire a corporate attorney, if you don't already have one.
- Consider hiring an attorney or consultant for yourself who specializes in executive compensation.
- Read your company's legal documents, whether they are by-laws or operating agreements. Highlight anything related to boards or advisors.

Chapter 6

ORGANIZE

We talked about the types and cadence of meetings in Chapter 4. Once you're ready to meet together as a board, the first item of business is creating the agenda for the meeting. The agenda frames the points of discussion and goals for the board meeting, and the way you approach it can produce an orderly discussion or a chaotic one.

GET IT TOGETHER

It takes time to pull the agenda together, and it starts with you, as the CEO, developing clarity regarding your business. Focusing on the board topics and prepping materials for the board members helps you clarify your business purpose and potential.

As you create the agenda for the meeting, keep in mind that this is a time when you will have everyone together. Take this opportunity to focus on high-priority matters and put the specifics you want to address on the agenda. For instance, "We're going to discuss next quarter's sales goals and strategies, which are outlined in the quarterly sales report." In this example, the quarterly sales report has already been sent to each board member. At the time of the meeting, each member is already aware of the details in the report and why they are significant. At the board meeting, as stated on the agenda, they will discuss and strategize regarding next quarter's sales goals.

Notice that neither a presentation nor full review of the report is taking place. The board meeting is not the time for long presentations of information. That is a passive activity. You want to provide preparatory information at least one week before your board meeting. Presentations can and should be included in this advance material. Your goal at the meeting is to convey what you need from the board: a discussion, a vote, etc.

Lead with specific language such as "This is the proposed change," as opposed to "We're voting on the agreement; here's the agreement." Prepping your board with comprehensive materials and discussing topics with board members individually in the days or weeks prior to the meeting will ensure that there are no surprises. Surprises lead to long, contentious board meetings. The more information you provide ahead of the meeting, as clearly and concisely as possible, the better the board members will be able to perform their job. Major changes or major issues are all worth discussing in advance with individual board members to get their insights.

During the board meeting, you discuss matters on which you need advising. Additionally, there may be specific actions the board needs to take, such as voting on compensation structure or approving a change to the way the company conducts business. Put these action items on the agenda as well. This focuses your meeting and your members toward accomplishing that goal. Keep in mind, you are checking in with each board member regularly. Utilize that communication time to get the thoughts of your team on these high-priority matters. The goal in all of the communication, prep, and delivery is to keep the actual board meeting concise and the agenda moving forward. Below is an example of a board agenda. As with any meeting, you'll create a custom agenda that facilitates the necessary discussion.

SAMPLE AGENDA

1. Call to order
2. Approval of board minutes from the previous meeting (sent with the board packet in advance)
3. Quarterly review
   a. Performance report (Sometimes it is helpful to provide a simple overview of whether something was achieved or not and provide the details as part of the board packet. Best practice is that goals should all be measurable rather than vague.)
   b. Next quarter's goals, which build upon the current performance with details provided in the board materials
4. Risk management
   a. Votes needed on Issue A
5. CEO report
   a. Discussion Item A
   b. Discussion Item B
6. Executive session
7. Adjournment

EXECUTIVE SESSION

Each board meeting should have an executive session. This is a session only for board members and excludes board observers and any non-board staff members. The CEO is often at this meeting. Most executive sessions are held at the end of the board meeting so that all other attendees can be dismissed. Some good reasons to hold an executive session would be to:

- Create a confidential atmosphere to discuss sensitive topics such as possible legal actions, terminating senior people, issues with investors, etc.

- Enhance the relationship among board members and with the CEO by focusing on the board itself as a core group. The executive session can be more relaxed because the group is smaller and conversations are more intimate.
- Connect with advisors such as the company attorney to discuss specific issues.

A consistent practice of holding an executive session after every meeting creates an atmosphere that builds trust. Also, if you have never held an executive session and then decide to hold one, it will set off alarm bells for staff and observers!

Important: The executive session comprises solely board members plus possibly the corporate counsel. The board meeting at-large may include outside invitees, such as key executives or staff members; guests, such as advisors; or other stakeholders.

AD HOC BOARD MEETINGS

Off-cycle board meetings can occur for a variety of reasons, and your attorney should include something flexible in your legal documents allowing you to call a board meeting anytime. Of course, you do not want to abuse this privilege, but in a situation where a vote needs to take place or an emergency occurs, you certainly should have the option to call your board together.

A board vote alone doesn't require a board meeting. You can hold votes electronically. You would hold a special board meeting to discuss an issue that cannot wait for the next meeting.

Use the weekly calls to prepare your board members for the topic of your off-cycle gathering so they already know what's coming. The point of calling an off-cycle board meeting is that you have an action the board needs to take immediately, before the next official meeting. Be clear on this action, and as always, provide as much information as you can ahead of time.

TOO MUCH INFORMATION

The message of advanced preparation is reiterated throughout the book, and sharing information is crucial to leading successful board meetings and managing the board effectively. I would be remiss, however, if I did not address the fact that there is such a thing as giving too much information, meaning pages of narrative, history, and statistics in advance. Active, vibrant board members struggle to find time to digest material from an overeager, oversharing CEO. Jess, an entrepreneur I know of, found herself in this situation. She had painstakingly prepared her materials and sent them well in advance, but the board meeting was frustrating and ineffective.

She had prepared far too much overly dense material for the board members to get through with their busy schedules. No one was prepared, everyone seemed slightly confused, and the typical bickering ensued. In this case, she might have chosen a more expeditious way to communicate that much detail.

Several CEOs I know have provided their business model to their board, which can be many, many tabs in a spreadsheet. Even with my love of spreadsheets and models, I found it overwhelming. In some cases it is helpful to get into the weeds, but most of the time it is information overload.

If there is a lot to convey, consider producing short, high-level video updates. This option is new to board prep, but a picture is truly worth a thousand words in this scenario. You can keep your audience interested and relay a lot of information in a five-to-ten-minute video. Video allows you to hit the high points and present your information in a short, clean way that considers your listeners. Often you can delegate this to the person on your team most familiar with the topic. This is a good way to introduce more members of your leadership team to your board.

If you add up all of the hours it takes to properly communicate with your board, it can be quite daunting. The truth is, communicating at this level actually *saves you time* in the end. If you are communicating regularly and frequently with your board members on all of the issues, your board meetings will be smooth and straightforward. Those who neglect this communication tend to have board meetings that go down rabbit hole after rabbit hole because people are getting information at different times and absorbing it in different ways, and they all collide at the board meeting. That is a scenario you want to intentionally avoid by regularly communicating with each board member.

If a topic has too much information to digest at the board meeting, creating a committee to address the issue then report back to the board may be the best way to handle it.

COMMITTEES

As your company starts to grow, the needs of the business will result in committees being formed within your board. Committees are pockets of board members who focus on a particular area of business, possibly to the extent of engaging the expertise of non-board members, if needed. There are countless possible committees, but CEOs of smaller companies may end up never adding more than one or two committees. As you grow, necessary committees will become apparent. Concentrate on present gaps that committees might fill. One of the earliest might be finance and/or compensation committees, as the largest expense for most companies is their payroll.

For large companies or nonprofits, many corporate documents are specific about which committees are needed and how they are to be established. For small companies, none of that is needed. Having the flexibility to form and disband committees will serve the company well. Ad hoc committees may form for a certain duration of time and then dissolve, such as a committee designed to oversee a possible merger or acquisition.

Like the board itself, committees have roles and reporting responsibilities.

COMMITTEE CHAIR

A committee needs to have a chair to be the organizer and focal point for the committee. That chair is ideally the liaison between the committee's work and the board chair. The chair should have relevant experience with the issues for the committee, such as having a CPA chair the audit committee. Not all committees need subject matter expertise, and an experienced board member is helpful.

COMMITTEE REPORTING

The committee should regularly report to the board chairperson. Don't use a board meeting for a committee report-out. First of all, it is boring. Second of all, reports should be shared before the meeting so members have time to digest the information then discuss important issues that move the company forward.

During the board meeting, the committee brings a particular action item to the table, especially if the board needs to vote. If we go back to a compensation committee as an example, they may have worked with the CEO to craft the policies and procedures for compensation, and the plan is ready to be voted on by the board. Prior to the board meeting, as part of the board packet, the summarized information from the committee is provided so that all board members have the key information they need for a discussion. The process is to bring it up at the board meeting, broader discussion ensues, and a vote takes place. If something as significant as compensation policy is on the table, there's going to be that full procedure of complete reporting beforehand, discussion at the board level, and then a vote. A simpler issue may only need minimal discussion before a vote because members will have had time to review materials before the meeting.

Large companies have a formal structure of committees, whereas small companies rely on ad hoc committees to address issues as they arise. As your company grows, you may decide to create committees for your board to focus on certain issues such as the following:

AUDIT COMMITTEE

CEOs of smaller companies do not need to establish an audit committee. You will not need an audit unless it's required for the kind of work you do, and your attorney or CPA will alert you to any legal requirements to do so. For instance, if your company receives certain grants or has certain kinds of government contracts, you may need an audit. Publicly traded companies require audits of financials by independent accountants. In these cases, an audit committee would be established to oversee the audit, identify the firm that will perform the job, and supervise the main accounting issues identified by the auditor.

Note that if you are planning to sell your company, especially as sales grow into the multimillions, companies that have a record of audited financials typically get a premium from an acquirer over those without this independent review. A history of audits can garner a better selling price.

COMPENSATION COMMITTEE

We've heard some examples of what a compensation committee does, but for the sake of clarity, the compensation committee approves the compensation policies of the company. This would include their cash, salary, bonus, and any incentive plans which may or may not include stock and stock options. The compensation committee approves appropriate levels of compensation for particular positions, approves policy, and brings those decisions to the board for a final vote.

An important role for board members in general, and compensation committees in particular, is to help the CEO access and analyze market data on salaries and benefits. Smaller companies may find it difficult to recruit talented people when the company is competing with larger, better resourced companies. A board can help a CEO navigate this by providing real data and a broader perspective.

GOVERNANCE AND NOMINATING

As you expand your board, you may want to have a couple of board members, perhaps with the help of other advisors, work to vet and bring forward board candidates. The governance part reviews compliance with certain laws governing the operations of the company. This will include making sure the shareholder agreements are in line with how you're operating. Nominating is all about recruiting board members, assigning committee members, and thinking about board leadership.

RISK MANAGEMENT

Companies face operational risks, and it is the board's responsibility to understand these risks. Risks range from sexual harassment to cyberhacking to the effects of climate change and a global pandemic. Risk management oversight can be an important contribution from board members who have varied and extensive experience, and it may be effective to break up and address the different risks separately.

EXIT

One of the most misunderstood aspects of business is how to successfully exit. In most cases, a successful exit means that a company gets sold to or merges with another company.

Most business owners do not understand how much work is involved in getting a company ready for sale and finding buyers. In fact, we often prefer to say that the "company was sold" because the onus on an exit is almost always on the company that is selling. It can take years to position a company in a way that attracts the right kinds of buyers. If you plan to sell your business in the next five years, you should be thinking about working toward that goal now. Having a subcommittee of people who have successfully worked on a company sale is incredibly valuable.

An organized company and organized board meetings are two sides of the same coin; each drives the other. After you learn the benefits of having a board of directors and participate in the board of your company, you may find yourself curious and ready to serve as a board member for another company. You've gained from the experience of others, and now is your opportunity to give back.

ACTION STEP: PRACTICE CREATING AN AGENDA

Look at your current business situation, and take the time to prepare an agenda as if you already have your board of directors.

- What business challenges arise?
- Where is your focus?
- How would you present this information, by report or video presentation?

Chapter 7

A
N
C
H
O

REFRESH AND RETURN

About two years ago, when Carly first created the board of her company, she wanted input on building out her team. She needed someone to take charge of order fulfillment, invoicing, and vendor relations. She sought guidance from the board with this in mind as the number-one priority. In turn, the board was a great assistance in helping her recruit and network, and she developed that team more quickly than she thought she would.

With her full staff in place, naturally, she wanted to keep them busy with expanded growth. She could now envision diversifying her product line and expanding into different geographical locations. When she tried to move the company in that direction, she realized most of the board was from her immediate community. That made sense when she was building up her local team, but now she needed one or two people who had experience with diversifying and geographic expansion. Carly revisited the first two steps of ANCHOR: she assessed her needs and began networking to add members to the board who could meet them.

GROW AND RENEW THE BOARD

If you're building a board to grow your business, you should expect that the business is going to grow. In turn, your advisory needs may evolve. As the priorities of your company change, you want to assess the members of the board for that change. Then, you begin the cycle all over again by refreshing your board. Term limits (discussed in Chapter 5) help to ease this process as it's clear when each board member's term will end. Refreshing is a bit different than the initial search when the CEO is on their own to identify and recruit the first board members. When you refresh, the existing board can assist, advise, and participate in the elimination, renewal, or addition of new members.

It's a good idea to start off with a smaller sized board of perhaps three including the CEO, and then after a few months expand the board to five and then maybe the following year add two more. This accomplishes several goals:

- It allows you to change and improve the onboarding process.
- Board members can assist the CEO to identify gaps and potential members to fill them.
- Set terms and staggered onboarding ensures you don't lose

all board members at one time. Overlapping board members is important for maintaining institutional knowledge.

RETURN THE FAVOR: BECOME A BOARD MEMBER

Natalie, one of the busiest CEOs I know, currently serves on two outside boards. When asked about her journey to serving on a board, she explained she began serving on boards when she was in graduate school and has been on a board ever since. She first served on a community nonprofit board that was designed to engage younger professionals. Through this work she met many business leaders in a variety of industries. Many of those people are still part of her network, and all of the boards she has been on since that time are the result of her connections made along the way. One of the boards she serves on is for a company with over $100 million in revenue. By serving on these different boards she was able to demonstrate her abilities, which led to more opportunities. She earned a reputation for being smart, hardworking, and a great collaborator. Her fellow and more senior board members presented her with each new board opportunity and at times tapped her for roles in their companies.

Notwithstanding her success, she's one of the most unassuming, humble people you'd ever meet, which proves you don't need to be brash, schmoozy, or pushy to be a successful networker.

Experienced business leaders know that there is a mountain of information that can't be found in any book, and they genuinely want to bestow this knowledge upon future industry professionals. Many successful business owners who sell or depart from their businesses are keen to serve on a board. As CEO you have been in the position to identify board members, and now you may want to pursue opportunities to sit on the other side of the table.

FIND THE RIGHT BOARD

A friend of mine, who is an extremely talented healthcare executive, was expressing her desire to serve on a board. I enthusiastically encouraged her. She was smart, had some unique healthcare industry experience, and cared deeply about her work and the people it affected. These attributes make great board participants. Therefore, I was stunned when she revealed that she had shown interest in board membership several times in the past and had even been interviewed a few times, but she had yet to be asked to actually serve. As we pondered this, we realized that she had no relationships with any of those boards' members. Before she could stand out as a rockstar candidate, she had to build those relationships as she had built other relationships: by asking for introductions from common connections, reaching out to meet at a conference, or having a lunch or coffee meeting.

Just as you sought out diverse board members when you were seeking a board, you want to use those same networking techniques to find the right board for you to serve. Assess skills and experience you have and who can benefit from them; network, whether locally or long-distance, to find those who need your expertise; and begin to reach out.

You may not realize how many professionals you come in contact with every day. Your accountant, lawyer, wealth manager, and everyday business contacts all have relevant networks and experience. Let these individuals know that you are looking to serve on a board of directors. If nothing else, I'll wager some interesting conversations will start, and paths forward will open up.

Of course, if you belong to any business associations, this creates an inroad into boards in your industry.

To determine what board is actually right for you, ask yourself these questions in relation to the company you're thinking of approaching:

1. What is the value or expertise that I bring to the company?
2. Is this value something the company needs?
3. Do they want this expertise?
4. Are the company size, markets, and team dynamics a fit for me?
5. What seat would I fill?
6. Do I want to see this company and CEO succeed? Why?
7. Will I be willing to use my social capital—my reputation, my connections—to help this company?

If you feel fairly certain that one day you'd like to participate in board service, start networking early. Those who recommend other people for boards are usually other board members and investors. You want to be top of mind when the nominating committee begins filling board seats.

Important: My experience has been that networking directly with board chairs or CEOs is more effective, however, large companies sometimes use recruiters to add to their pipeline of candidates, so you could reach out to recruiters to express interest in serving.

Although they account for only a small portion of board place-ment, many companies are facing pressure to add diversity to their boards, and a recruiter might be looking for you!

APPLICATION OR NOMINATION?

Typically, it's the CEO or the board who actively look for members, so an application process is possible but not common. For smaller businesses, the CEO and board chair will make independent decisions regarding who will be on the board. Slightly larger boards will have a nominating commit-tee actively looking for board members. Large boards might have an outside consultant or recruiter doing that work.

THE INTERVIEW PROCESS

You want to get to know the board members before sitting down to an interview for a board seat. Likely, the CEO will grant you the chance for some social interaction beforehand. The process involves multiple interviews with the CEO, the board members, and possibly other members of the executive staff. Expect a lot of conversation.

NOW YOU'RE A MEMBER

Just as the CEO must prepare materials to share with the board at least one week in advance of the meeting, it is expected that you, as a board member, read them with a mind toward taking action on the contents. It's your responsibility to offer solutions and guidance to the company. Come prepared to proactively respond to the meeting reports. If you have data, studies, experts, experience, or anything relevant to governing the situation outlined therein, be ready to present and discuss it. Notice, once again, that no one is reading materials at the meeting; the board meeting is the time to respond and take action.

Part of being prepared is understanding that your social capital is expected to be shared with your CEO. Before accepting any seat, examine how comfortable you are leveraging your social capital for the company whose board you'll be joining. The connections each board member brings to the company are essential for their goals to be met. If you're not sure that you want to connect them, then you might want to rethink being on that board.

REVERSE ONBOARDING

I was excited to join the board of a young organization because of their high-growth potential and the impact I believed I could bring to their board. I attended the first meeting as a guest, and it was report-out after report-out for over an hour. It was boring and ineffectively run, in my opinion, and I did not see the growth I thought this company was capable of.

I learned from that experience that when I am being considered by a CEO, it is also my chance to reverse onboard them. During onboarding, you are receiving company reports, executive profiles, and the bios of co-board members. This is your chance to be sure that the company and board style fits your temperament, commitment level, and expertise. Find out during this time who you will be working with and the expectations they have for you in your board role, and take a good look at how your area of expertise can be applied.

RESIGNING FROM THE BOARD

I was once on a board and I strongly disagreed with the company's decision to extend the length of the contract of the CEO. The rest of the board felt that this was the right path, and I knew that since I did not support that decision, I would then also not be an effective board member. Board members must go along with the decisions made by the company and by the board. If they cannot live with the decision, it's best to resign. I decided to resign from that board because that decision going forward would be reflected in everything that we did.

I have been on boards where members keep reminding everyone that they voted against a particular issue. That is not constructive. As a board member, you cannot undermine the path forward. When the conflict prohibits progress, you may decide you are not a good fit for that board after all. Resign if you cannot live with a decision that has been made.

If, instead, you feel you can no longer meet your board obligations, you can choose to resign from your position. The number-one reason for board resignation is that the member miscalculated the time commitment needed to properly contribute. You'll be on call for monthly board updates plus the quarterly and yearly meetings. If you choose to serve on a committee, that will mean dedicating additional time. Surprisingly, smaller boards often take more time than a larger board, and a small board for a small company takes the most time commitment of all. Be aware of this as you consider board service, and calculate your own time wisely.

Whatever the reason, if you feel you can no longer be an effective board member, it's always good practice to open lines of communication with the CEO about the difficulty, if she is not already aware. Prepare a professional resignation letter, and be sure the board chair receives a copy.

Another option, rather than outright resignation, is to request a leave of absence. In the case of health situations, for instance, there may be a recovery period involved, after which time you can return to board service. Be candid with your CEO, if this becomes the case. Make arrangements with her to have your subject matters covered by another member, if you're able, and try to give a specific time frame that she can expect to be without your participation.

* * *

As a former soccer player, I believe in the mantra that "the game is the best teacher." The same is true for serving on boards. You will learn so much by serving on a board, and you'll bring that experience to your work as CEO and to your own company's board of directors.

Your board should grow with your company. Keep this in mind as you build invaluable business relationships. You'll meet people you'd like to invite to your board, but perhaps they are a better fit when your company has grown. I've seen countless situations where an acquaintance becomes an advisor, who then becomes a board member. Whichever phase you're in, whether you're looking for board members or looking to serve on a board, you should be prepared to weather difficulties on the journey.

ACTION STEP: WHERE WOULD YOU LIKE TO SERVE?

Take a few moments to answer these questions as honestly as you can.
Feel free to expand your answers in a notebook you can refer back to.

- List the types of boards you have an interest in serving on:
- What superpower of yours do you want to strengthen?
- How, specifically, can you begin to network in those areas, even now?

Chapter 8

LEAN ON YOUR BOARD

Having an effective board can help catapult your business and you as a CEO to great success. At various times in your company's journey, the board will deal with difficult circumstances. The situation may be created by an external crisis such as an economic crash, a natural disaster, or a pandemic. Or the crisis may occur internally, for example the board is not highly functioning because it has some bad actors. I have some experience in internal and external situations, so I hope you can learn the lessons from these experiences.

FACING A CRISIS

A CEO agreed to give a specific, individual investor a board seat, and they negotiated that he would remain there until the company valuation reached a certain dollar amount of capital raised, which would be far into the future. The CEO was a first-time founder and didn't know how problematic this could be and how necessary it was that she needed to protect herself. I know she had a good corporate attorney, but he failed her in this situation.

First-time founders are often so challenged by raising capital from investors that they give concessions to these investors that have lasting, negative impacts. Sometimes they agree to sell too much of their company for the capital that is being put in, and sometimes—as in this case—they agree to allow someone to serve on the board without recourse to remove them.

This often happens because there is a "scarcity mindset" where entrepreneurs are so thankful for investment that they cede their power. Instead, they should have the confidence that their company will be a highly profitable investment and they are inviting investors to share in the success. It's a hard mindset to maintain in the fundraising process.

In this particular case, the company went through challenging times, and this particular board member turned out to be verbally abusive. He would send the CEO berating and taunting emails that criticized her decisions and undermined her confidence. He was a bully. She did not share these emails until much later when the company was in a deep crisis.

From the outside, I could see that the board was not functioning properly, and that was no doubt caused by the lack of cohesion of the group. Here are some examples of the dysfunction:

- The board did not provide any assistance when the company was looking to raise their next fundraising round. The inexperienced and unsupported CEO only had one investment company interested, and when that company pulled out at the last minute, it left the company in a deep cash crisis. A good board helps a CEO keep an eye on the financials and mitigates risks.

- The board lacked a member with financial expertise, and the company was understaffed in this area. Neither the CEO nor the board understood the financials well enough to see the problems arising. They did not understand the unit costs of their product line.

- The company undertook several operational changes, and there was no expertise on the board or on the staff to push back on the supply chain issues that the changes caused.

Unfortunately, the CEO suffered in silence and thought that there was nothing she could do to remove the disruptive member because she had agreed to the terms. He was a harassing figure for years, threatening a lawsuit if she tried to kick him off the board. The only removal process he would accept was a full buyout of his interest, but that was precious capital that nobody felt comfortable returning to him. While that board member was being rude and offensive, the rest of the board did not notice that the company did not have the proper financial controls in place to understand the true economics of its products. The toxic environment had a ripple effect throughout the business.

By the time new board members joined and learned about his behavior and all of the problems at the company, it was too late. The CEO was burned out and wanted to be replaced, and the company was faltering. In the end, that company went out of business, and millions of dollars of investment were lost.

Lessons learned:

- Always have a code of conduct that allows you to remove a board member for bad behavior.
- Negotiate approval of who represents investors on your board. Have your investor provide a couple of names and interview those people.
- Conduct a skills assessment of the board of directors to identify their gaps. Compare that with a skills assessment of your company. Seek a board member to fill the gap, and talk to the CEO about gaps on the staff.
- Make risk management a routine part of your board meetings.
- First-time founders should never be the board chairperson.

This story was a terrible experience for the founder, the company, and investors. It was a tremendous learning experience for me. Oftentimes we learn the most from negative experiences.

HANDLING DISAGREEMENTS

Disagreements at the board level can happen over something as simple as a hiring strategy or as complex as the new location of your manufacturing facility. If you, as the CEO, have a disagreement at the board level, you will have to decide how serious the disagreement is to you. As CEO you need to understand where the line is between getting advice and counsel from your board and getting approval from them. Large decisions, especially ones with large financial implications, are typically matters that the board needs to approve. Other topics, such as specific hiring choices and marketing strategies, are more informational and good for discussion.

If a board member disagrees with a matter, they too will have to decide on the severity of the situation and how to deal with the disagreement. If you, as CEO, see a board member who stands too far in disagreement and they aren't voluntarily stepping down, you need to take steps to remove the disruptor.

WHEN A BOARD MEMBER ISN'T WORKING OUT

If you have made a mistake and brought somebody onto your board who isn't working out, typically there are four possible causes: the person doesn't have enough time; they have a rude or disruptive personality; they're not engaged; or they're just not suited to your environment.

Rude or Disruptive Behavior

I've already described a situation previously where the board member was a bully and should have been removed long ago. There are other types of disruptive behavior. A common one involves institutional investors.

Venture capital funds have a set lifespan for their funds, typically seven years, although that term can be extended. First they raise capital from outside investors, then they take a couple of years to invest in companies to create their portfolio (often of eight to ten companies). This investment may include initial investment and then additional "follow on" investments. Then, the venture capital fund hopes that there is a return on investment before the end of the term of their fund. It is difficult to predict if the timing will work out, and sometimes investors can push a company to consider a sale or merger before it is ready.

One of my investments had a board member who represented a fund that was invested in the company, and that fund was about to hit its end date (again, the fund has options such as extending the date or selling its position to another investor). In this case, the board member started to push the company aggressively toward selling. This caused the CEO to spend a lot of time talking to potential suitors, and as we all expected, nothing happened because the company was too small to garner serious attention. They certainly could not return capital to investors in this scenario. The board member continued to push this agenda, motivated by the fund rather than keeping the best interests of the company foremost. This is an important reminder that board members are there to serve the best interests of the company and not their own investor interests. That board member eventually resigned, but countless hours were wasted on this effort, and the other board members should have stopped this behavior earlier by reminding the board of their responsibility to the company and not specific investors.

It's doubtful that any CEO encountering an outright difficult person would allow them onto the board, so how does this happen? It's been my experience that outright disruptive individuals are usually representatives of investors. You absolutely do not have to tolerate any type of abuse, and you should boldly expose anyone who is making disparaging remarks, unwanted sexual advances, or threats against your company. Document any mistreatment, and immediately share it with the rest of the board. Have an established code of conduct and stick by it.

If the CEO in my earlier story had spoken up the first time she received a rude email and she had a code of conduct to point to, it's possible that her controlling investor would have been removed. She clearly did not feel supported enough by the other members of her board to bring this to their attention. Once again, be careful to work with your lawyer to ensure that you are never without recourse in this kind of a situation.

Disengaged or Overcommitted

One CEO I worked with had a thriving company, and she included several experts on the board. As a new investor, I set out to get to know the board members as part of my due diligence on the company. I met a board member who remains to this day the most lackluster, uninformed board member I've ever encountered. He confessed to not having a professional rapport with our CEO outside of the board meetings, which he did not attend regularly. By my calculation that meant that he talked with her two, possibly three times a year. When asked about the company's development, he responded with kind words about the CEO, saying that she was a great "go-getter" and a "nice person," but he did not know any of the elements of her business that he should have been well versed in.

A person who holds a board seat with this level of disengagement wastes their and the CEO's time. The CEO needs counsel and guidance, and the board members should give her that.

Also, this type of obvious disinterest may influence other board members, leading to a lackluster board.

In this case, the young, new CEO was also the chair of the board. Have we noticed a pattern? If she had a strong board chair, the other board member would have been coached out or possibly re-engaged. (I suspect the former.)

You may have been persuasive in getting someone to join your board, and maybe they conceded out of a sense of obligation; or it could be that they wanted to be a part of your vision, but because their time is so limited, they are unable to keep their commitment to the board. In most cases, people who have some sense of personal responsibility will be aware and apologetic for not participating to the extent that others do. It may be a relief when you suggest that they resign from the board. If you want to keep the person engaged, you could ask them to be an uncompensated advisor.

Getting to know someone as an informal advisor first is a great way to see if they would make a good, engaged board member.

Not Suited to Your Board

Mei, the CEO of a small financial technology company, was thrilled when she found out that a senior finance officer of a multibillion-dollar player in her field agreed to be on the board. The enthusiasm was mutual, and the board was eager to work with this giant in the industry. After several months of trying to make progress, Mei came to understand that her new board member's expertise was in large corporations, and she was unfamiliar with the inner workings of a small, fast-growing company. Mei needed someone who was flexible and nimble but also understood the roadblocks ahead. The experienced executive did not have those skills.

Those who are several steps ahead, but not leaps ahead, of your current business situation make effective board members. A board that is guiding a $5 million company should have at least one member who has experience handling similar revenue and has grown to a larger company. Practicality should dictate that business leaders who are too far ahead might not be able to relate to the CEO's needs. If prospective board members have only been part of billion-dollar companies, they may not understand the day-to-day existence of the CEO of a multimillion dollar company.

Oftentimes a CEO may want someone on their board for the credentials that they signal. That is a trap that many entrepreneurs fall into. They want to have members from big companies, well-known brands, or even celebrities on their board. These people often don't have the time to commit to a board of directors and, as described in the previous story, they don't have the appropriate frame of reference to provide the support a growing, small company needs.

It is tempting to add those big names to your board, but I recommend that you designate them as advisors and showcase them and their involvement in strategic ways. Here are some ideas on effective ways to utilize them:

- Have them make introductions for you.
- Arrange speaking engagements such as a fireside chat between you and them.

- If you sponsor a conference or webinar series, invite them to keynote.
- Get their endorsement of your products or services or of you personally.

Juanita, a CEO in the homecare industry, found herself in a similar spot, with a board that wasn't suited to her. She wanted to soar, expand into all kinds of healthcare training and facilitation. The board, however, seemed more interested in maintaining the status quo. She needed a board that had a bigger vision for her company, and she had to eventually replace those trying to limit her with those who were more aligned with her expansion plans.

She was ultimately able to connect with investors for her next round of investment, and those investors shared her vision for the wider market. It took until her new round to swap out some board members. It took a lot of diplomacy to manage that transition, but with the help of some board members and her new investors, she was successful at bridging to the new vision.

EXTERNAL CRISES

The CEO's board can and should help them plan for crisis situations before they even happen. During an unforeseen crisis, a board can also stand as a solid guiding force, as happened to a colleague of mine in 2008. She lost a large amount of revenue during the financial crisis when her key customers halted all projects. She hesitated to tell her team because she felt that it was her responsibility to offer solutions, and she had none. She thought that as leader, she was responsible to lead her team out of disaster. The stress was overwhelming, causing sleepless nights and daytime distraction.

One of the board members firmly encouraged her to discuss this crisis with her team. She counseled the CEO to trust her staff and to allow them to brainstorm some solutions with her. That action completely turned the company around; a potentially devastating situation unified her team even more than they already were. They were able to weather that difficult storm.

A CEO may not want to think about total property loss, sickness, or her own death, but board members should be proactive in planning for those types of risks. By "planning," I mean that you and your board put a succession plan in writing in case you are incapacitated in any way. In cases of sickness or temporary leave of absence, the chief operating officer or chief financial officer may step in to fill that role. In fact, you should think about that for every role at your company. Are your processes well documented so that someone could step into another person's role with minimal disruption?

If the CEO is the board chair (and they should not be, as I have said) another board member needs to step into that role. However you choose to resolve an emergency, a documented plan must be in place so the board and executive staff know exactly how to execute it. I recommend following Gino Wickman's three step process: Identify, Document, Package, as outlined in his book *Traction: Get a Grip on Your Business.*

Many companies have been thrown into complete turmoil by the sudden death or illness of an executive.

The pandemic showed us that many people could quite capably work from home, but there were also problems such as the custody of sensitive documents, the use of company laptops by family members, and the overall lack of privacy. When you document your company's processes, you need to identify sensitive elements and implement plans for maintaining privacy.

In the pandemic we also saw tremendous problems in the supply chain. There were long delays for certain products, and the costs of others skyrocketed. In these cases, having a board focused on short- and medium-term solutions can be incredibly valuable.

One of my portfolio companies was already talking in January 2020 (!) about taking steps to manage the supply chain issues caused by the pandemic, because she could see that her suppliers in China were being severely affected. She decided that the conservative thing to do would be to buy extra components in February 2020 so that her product assembly in the United States would have what they needed. That strategy required more capital than she forecasted. She knew her per unit costs of her product, so she knew how much margin she had to use. As a result, her company minimized their disruptions.

The board should think and guide the conversation about the risk of natural disaster or theft and proactively look to protect the company. A fire or hurricane could damage physical company property, or thieves could break in and steal the computers. Critical paper records should be kept in a fireproof safe or stored safely offsite. The risk and threat of cyber theft should be addressed; given the amount of data most companies store in the cloud, sufficient backup is an ongoing concern.

A board member with risk management experience can advise the company on the appropriate type and quantity of property insurance to cover rebuild costs in the event of a worst-case scenario. The board should be asking questions, and you, as the CEO, are responsible to implement solutions.

THE BENEFITS OF A BOARD DURING A CRISIS

At the beginning of the 2020 shutdown, CEOs and boards of directors could see that a crisis was unfolding and with that would be a lot of market uncertainty. As a board member advising on finances, I knew that my portfolio companies each needed to make sure that they held eighteen months of cash.

Every company needed to reconfigure their models to reflect an ever-changing environment. All companies took measures to decrease their "burn rate," which is the amount of expenses a company incurs net of any incoming revenue. If you take the amount of cash and receivables you have and then divide that amount by the monthly burn amount, you can see how many months you have available to you. This is also referred to as your "runway."

In early 2020 every company and every board was thinking about how to decrease costs. Many looked to terminate or renegotiate leases when everyone was working from home.

One CEO planned layoffs, but the board advised her to think about accomplishing the same goal of reducing expenses by asking everyone to take a 20 percent pay cut. People in this economy were agreeable to take the pay cut and still have the job.

There were many examples of how companies managed, and the key point is that these efforts were typically a group undertaking. The most stressed out CEOs I knew had a small executive team and a small—or no—board.

When people are in crisis, it is important to bring a diverse group of perspectives to bear on solving the problems. Management research repeatedly shows that a diverse team will come up with more creative solutions than a couple of smart people will.

You may meet more frequently during these times, say biweekly, because typically budgets, customer strategy, and operations must all be reimagined during unstable periods.

Your diverse board should include members who have experienced multiple economic downturns and a variety of crises. Lean heavily on their expertise, because things will come up in a crisis that you may never have had to deal with, such as closing offices, laying people off, or downsizing whole portions of your company. Having that board support may make the difference between successfully weathering the situation or not.

Part of getting through a crisis is simply acknowledging that CEOs and board members are all human. In some cases, as with illnesses, they're dealing with the crisis in the business, then they deal with it again in their own professional life. One executive I know who was instrumental in 2020 in saving several jobs for the company he sat on a board for, but he could not do the same for his own company. It was painful to know that he had to lay off most of his own staff.

During a crisis, a board member is under no obligation to financially bail out the company where they serve. They can help the company secure financing from other sources, but a board member, even if they're an investor, is not required to bail out a company in crisis.

Important: Crisis points often are the best time to invest in a company. After the 2008 financial crisis, companies who survived were some of the most successful companies to emerge. In the early days of the 2020 pandemic, we saw that the valuations for companies (the price you pay to invest) faced immediate downward pressure. As investors, we were able to consider companies that were too expensive to invest in during 2019 because CEOs prioritized bringing in more capital over pushing up valuations. "Cash is king" is a truism. Maybe we should say that cash is queen?

MAKING A PLAN

No company avoids crises entirely, but planning ahead can help manage the risk and create a cushion for damage control. Plenty of research offers insights on effective decision-making. As part of the code of conduct of the board of directors, you can also include guidelines for making decisions as a group, especially when faced with a crisis.

Discuss how you are going to decide the outcome of a big decision. In some cases, as CEO you will make the ultimate decision after gathering input from the board members. In other situations, you may gather all information and bring it to a vote on a specific day. Map out the process to define who will be responsible for researching certain aspects of the decision, how that research will be disseminated, and when the vote will take place.

Remember, a large percentage of people like to consider information before making a decision. As described earlier, know whether you and your board members are "ponderers" and make sure that everyone has the information they need in advance.

You began this journey by planning for the type of board that would best serve your company. Now that you have a board, plan with them for the future success of the company.

Remember at the beginning of this book, I visualized that you were standing on a hill, looking across to your destination. You need advice, guidance, and support to make the journey. Having a board of directors will guide you through the valleys and tough crossing, and they will also share in your success with you when you reach new heights.

I joined a board a few years ago, and the CEO faced many challenges with investors who didn't see or share her vision and challenged her expertise. I witnessed how condescending and ill-informed these investors were and how demoralizing it was for the CEO. She needed investment to grow her team from a handful of part-time employees, but the investment landscape looked bleak. One board member introduced her to a funder who another board member also knew. With two people vouching for the CEO, that funder reached out to his network, and multiple investors, who were enthusiastic about her business, engaged and invested. Through the right connections—after much disappointment and rejection—that CEO found investors who shared her vision and opened the door to other investors. It wasn't all smooth negotiations, but the journey has led her to grow her staff tenfold and position her company to become the leader in its industry.

It has been so rewarding for me to see how well she has done so far, and there is much more success ahead for her and her team. The successes have been even more enjoyable for me because I was part of the difficult times as well.

Another company that I have advised for several years recently had an incredibly successful launch of a new product line, and the CEO was featured on one of the morning news programs. I remember when she needed a bridge loan to make payroll because investors were slow to make their investments. I also remember when she was doing her early fundraising while she was almost nine months pregnant. I have always admired her grit, and it gives me such joy to see her succeed.

Being part of that type of transformation is incredibly rewarding for me—and a reason that I continue to serve on boards.

ACTION STEP: MAKE A PLAN

- Write a code of conduct and share with your staff and board.
- Outline a delegation or "power of attorney" plan in case of your own unexpected absence. This is especially important for your company's banking.
- Have a planning day to go through some doomsday scenarios and document your processes.
- Perhaps test run your plan by taking a proper vacation without email or calls to the office. It is an excellent idea.

CONCLUSION

It has truly been my pleasure to spend time with you on your journey toward business growth. I hope that this book demystified building a board and showed you how it can be your secret sauce for success. My mission is to open up the world of board guidance to you as an entrepreneur. I encourage you to take each step slowly and think about each element carefully and deliberately.

As I search my own thoughts in closing the book, I'm full of hope and confidence in your ability to achieve the next level of success—and the next after that. In summary, ANCHOR yourself:

A—Assess your superpower and discover those that you lack.

N—Network to find people with the superpowers you need.

C—Communicate weekly, monthly, and quarterly with your board members, and stay in touch with possible future prospects.

H—Honor your legal duty.

O—Organize your company's talking points to move the conversation forward.

R—Refresh your board as you grow; return the favor by becoming a board member yourself.

Throughout the book, we've stressed the importance of hearing and collecting differing viewpoints. Practically speaking, this strategy of gathering diverse advisors is meant to give you the best competitive business edge.

Enjoy the journey!

RESOURCES

Organization and accountability:

Read the book *Traction: Get a Grip on Your Business* by Gino Wickman.

At my company The Impact Seat, as well as at some of our portfolio companies, we use the framework from *Traction* to organize how we set goals and measure success. Find free resources at eosworldwide.com.

Time management:

For an eye-opening analysis of how people really spend their time and how you might want to think differently about it, read *168 Hours: You Have More Time Than You Think* by Laura Vanderkam.

Decision-making:

How Women Decide: What's True, What's Not, and What Strategies Spark the Best Choices by Therese Huston provides interesting research on how people (not only women) make decisions in diverse groups.

Board training and networking:

Women2Boards, https://women2boards.com

50/50 Women on Boards, https://www.5050wob.com

Athena Alliance (https://athenaalliance.com) was helpful with information on board compensation.

ACKNOWLEDGMENTS

So many of us aspire to write a book, and I think the biggest misconception for me was that I just needed to hunker down and put pen to paper. The reality is that mobilizing a whole team of people, to help you in big ways and small, makes the process so much more enjoyable and manageable. Gee, that sounds like my advice for starting a board.

My deepest appreciation goes to my team at The Impact Seat. Thank you, Cheryl Contee, for being the force behind making me take the plunge from just talking about a book to actually writing a book. You blazed the path for me to follow with your own successful book *Mechanical Bull*. Cheryl, your relentless positivity was a blessing during this process.

Thank you, Gabby De La Cruz, for your keen eye and judgment about everything from the cover design to the marketing campaign. I appreciate how you are always thinking several steps ahead.

A very special thank you, Lisa Jessogne, for safeguarding my time while keeping us all on track. You coined the term "For Sanity" to create space in my often hectic calendar. Without your support and project management skills, we would not have enjoyed the journey and kept to our timetable (as well as we could, anyway).

Thank you, Dr. Teresa Nelson, my fellow co-founder of The Impact Seat. Your intellectual leadership on the issues around diversity, teams, entrepreneurship, and decision-making formed the foundation for many of the assessments in this book. Thank you, Teresa, for the hours we have spent over the years discussing the advantages of diverse teams and the management science behind how and why diverse teams win. Thank you for your friendship. I am so glad to have Jasmine Montanez building on this incredible work.

And of course, I have learned so much about applying theory to practice by serving on boards myself. I've worked with so many CEOs over the years that I cannot mention them all here, but there are several standouts.

A huge thank you to Kim Folsom, CEO of Founders First Capital Partners, for inviting me to serve on your board. You have served as an inspiration for many of the best practices in this book. I've been in awe of your tenacity and resilience for years, and I am glad to support you as a leader.

Thank you to Trish Costello and my fellow board members Judith Rodin and Chantell Preston. Judith, you've been a role model in how a chair should think about governance and fiduciary responsibilities. Serving with you, Chantell, has been a pleasure as you bring your different experiences to the board, and that has taught me a lot. Portfolia CEO Trish Costello, under your leadership I've seen how a visionary CEO pulls together a vast network to harness a range of talents to create a truly innovative company.

Thank you to my Scribe team, particularly Barbara Boyd, for coming up with the concept of the ANCHOR and at times doing some major surgery on this book's contents. Every draft you edited brought the book closer to my voice. I appreciate your talents.

Thank you to Kathleen McQuiggan of Artemis Financial Advisors. You are one of the most strategic, forward-thinking people I know. I am glad for your judicious counsel and friendship. When I see how far I've been able to take my vision, I have you to thank for your advice and support.

Thank you to Lynn Loacker, partner at Davis Wright Tremaine, for giving me an opportunity to test out some of the assessments in this book on the cohort of entrepreneurs in her Project W's Women Entrepreneurs Bootcamp.

Thank you, Karen Cone, your board experience was incredibly valuable when I was crafting the sections on board compensation. Thank you to the Masters VC leaders Anne Kennedy and Gillian Muessig for giving me early support to pursue this effort.

And where would I be without my good friends to keep me going? Eve Ward, thank you for always being up for a late afternoon chat at a café when we're both in town. Your journey with your company Bond and Des Voeux provided me with so many key insights.

Laurel McConville and Tara Bellucci, thank you for sustaining me during the pandemic and all our collective ups and downs. You two introverts keep teaching me how to manage diversity. I promise I won't make you come to any book launch parties.

Kit Murray Maloney, you've been on several entrepreneurial journeys, but it is your superpower of being a "sales whisperer" that inspired my thinking on that concept.

Thank you to my colleagues at Astia. I've been a founding member of Astia Angels since 2014 and have not only learned a lot from this collegial group of investors, but I've also had a damn good time, too. Thank you to Sharon Vosmek, CEO of Astia. For years we have talked about the importance of a strong board of directors and how it is essential for successful companies, and sometimes those lessons were learned the hard way. Fortunately, the good has been outweighing the bad! Thank you to Victoria Pettibone, managing director of Astia, for your almost encyclopedic knowledge of investments and constant push for good governance for our portfolio companies. Thank you, Karen Drexler, my fellow Astia Angel investor, whom I have watched serve as a board member for many years at different companies. You've been a role model for me.

Thank you, Kathryn Finney of Genius Guild, for your perspective on how to support nascent innovative ventures.

A huge heartfelt thank you Natalia Oberti Noguera, founder of Pipeline Angels, for challenging me and my fellow investors to demand our seat at the table. You consistently pressed us to serve on boards as a necessary element of successful investing. You've launched the investing career of so many women, and I am grateful for your life-changing program.

I'd also like to thank Alison Jones for inspiring me through her podcast *The Extraordinary Business Book Club*. Listening on a weekly basis to the journeys of other authors has been a helpful resource on other great business books and taught me what to expect on this journey.

And finally, thank you to my family. I am so lucky to have you in my life. None of you will probably ever read this book, anyway. Well, maybe this page.

ABOUT THE AUTHOR

Investor, economist, and entrepreneur BARBARA CLARKE enjoys interacting with professionals who believe in creating diverse teams to drive innovation and business success. Called "The Force," Barbara fuels change in the entrepreneurial eco-system, stimulates growth in early stage tech startups, and boosts organizational excellence with her investment exper-tise and global insights.

Co-founder and president of The Impact Seat, Barbara has been investing in emerging technologies, including medical devices, for a decade. To date, Barbara has invested in more than sixty companies and twelve funds in North America and Europe. She has been creating opportunities for under-represented entrepreneurs by investing in companies that are either led by women of color or have women on their funding teams—even before it became fashionable to do so. As a key member of the investment community, she also advises entrepreneurs and innovators on launching companies, accessing capital, and leveraging the international network of investors. To date, Barbara has been a part of three successful IPOs: Tivic Health, Athena SPAC, and RenovoRX.

Barbara serves on several boards, including Portfolia, an investment fund focused on women as venture capitalists; Founders First Capital Partners, an accelerator and finance firm that invests in a diverse group of founders; and Boost, an artificial intelligence (AI) platform using computer vision technology acquired by Arria NLG in 2021.

In 2021, Barbara launched The Impact Seat Foundation, which strives to create a world in which women, particularly women of color, succeed as business leaders. The Foundation provides rich resources, develops cutting-edge programming, and creates an ecosystem that sparks exponential growth. One of the initiatives of the Foundation will be to help CEOs launch their own boards of directors.

Prior to launching The Impact Seat, Barbara spent more than a decade in management consulting firms, including KPMG and PwC, and launched a nationwide nonprofit to support grieving children. She holds a bachelor's degree in quantitative economics from Tufts University and master's in international economics and finance from Brandeis University. A polyglot, she speaks several languages, including German, French, and Italian.

When she is not scoping out promising startups to invest in, Barbara enjoys exploring new cities, supporting local artists, and listening to alternative/indie rock.

CPSIA information can be obtained
at www.ICGtesting.com
Printed in the USA
JSHW031907200522
26062JS00003B/15